D0618308

HOUGHTON MIFFLIN HARCOURT

TEXAS JOURNEYS

Program Authors

James F. Baumann · David J. Chard · Jamal Cooks
J. David Cooper · Russell Gersten · Marjorie Lipson
Lesley Mandel Morrow · John J. Pikulski · Héctor H. Rivera
Mabel Rivera · Shane Templeton · Sheila W. Valencia
Catherine Valentino · MaryEllen Vogt

Consulting Author
Irene Fountas

 HOUGHTON MIFFLIN HARCOURT
School Publishers

ISBN 10:   0-54-724080-5
ISBN 13:   978-0-54-724080-0

23456789 - 0868 – 18 17 16 15 14 13 12 11 10

Hello, Reader!

Each day you are becoming a better reader. Good for you!

The stories in this book will take you to the sea, the jungle, and the desert. You will see animals that are furry, scaly, slinky, feathered, striped, and spotted. You will even read about sea slugs!

Get ready to read new words, visit new places, and learn about the world around us!

Sincerely,

The Authors

Unit 3

Nature Near and Far

Big Idea It's a big, wonderful world.

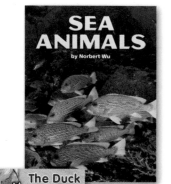

Lesson 11

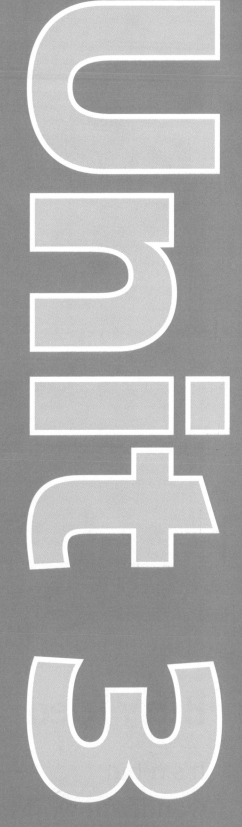

Nature
Near and Far

Unit 3

Big Idea

It's a big, wonderful world.

Selections

Readers' Theater

9

✔ **WORDS TO KNOW**
HIGH-FREQUENCY WORDS

cold

where

blue

live

far

their

little

water

Vocabulary
Reader

Context
Cards

TEKS 1.3H identify/read high-frequency
words; **ELPS** 1F use accessible language to
learn new language; 3B expand/internalize initial
English vocabulary

10

Words to Know

● Read each Context Card.

● Make up a new sentence
that uses a blue word.

1
cold
This ocean water is
very cold.

2
where
Sharks live where the
ocean is deep.

3 blue

Today the ocean water looks blue.

4 live

Whales live in all the oceans of the world.

5 far

Squid swim far below the ocean's surface.

6 their

Their home is by the ocean.

7 little

Many little fish live in the ocean.

8 water

Some people take photos in the water.

Background  Read Together

✔ **WORDS TO KNOW**   At Home in the Sea

1. Some animals live in warm, blue seas.

2. Other animals live in icy cold water.

3. How do sea animals get their food?

4. Some animals swim far to get food.

5. Some fish stay where plants grow.

6. Big fish may eat little fish.

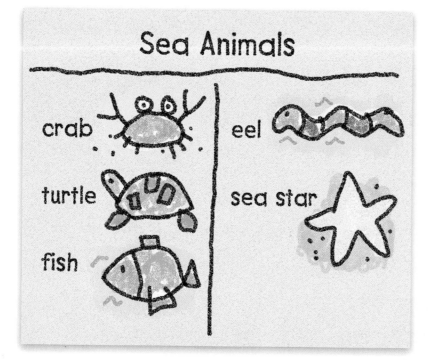

Name more big and little sea animals.

12

TEKS 1.4C establish purpose/monitor comprehension; **1.13** identify topic/explain author's purpose; **RC-1(A)** establish reading purposes; **ELPS 1E** internalize new basic/academic language; **4F** use visual/contextual/peer/teacher support to read/comprehend texts

Comprehension

Read Together

✓ **TARGET SKILL** Author's Purpose

Authors write for many reasons. They write stories to make you laugh. They write nonfiction selections to give information and help you learn things. Good readers think about why an author writes.

As you read **Sea Animals**, figure out why the author wrote and what he wants to tell you.

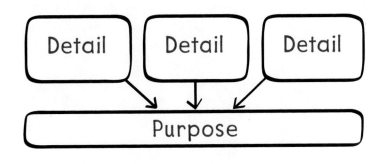

Detail | Detail | Detail → Purpose

JOURNEYS DIGITAL **Powered by** DESTINATIONReading®
Comprehension Activities: Lesson 11

SEA ANIMALS
by Norbert Wu

✔ WORDS TO KNOW

cold	far
where	their
blue	little
live	water

✔ TARGET SKILL

Author's Purpose Tell why an author writes.

✔ TARGET STRATEGY

Analyze/Evaluate Tell how you feel about the text, and why.

GENRE

Informational text gives facts about a topic.

TEKS 1.13 identify topic/explain author's purpose; **RC-1(F)** make connections to experiences/texts/community; **ELPS 4D** use prereading supports to comprehend texts; **4K** employ analytical skills to demonstrate comprehension

Meet the Author and Photographer

Norbert Wu

Norbert Wu's job as a nature photographer is exciting, but it can be dangerous. While taking photos of sea creatures, Mr. Wu has been attacked by sharks and trapped in an underwater cave. Check out his work in the book **Fish Faces**.

SEA ANIMALS

written and photographed by Norbert Wu

Essential Question

Why do authors write stories?

What is it like to live in the sea?

Lots of animals and plants live here.

giant jellyfish

The animals can be big.

clown fish

They can be little.

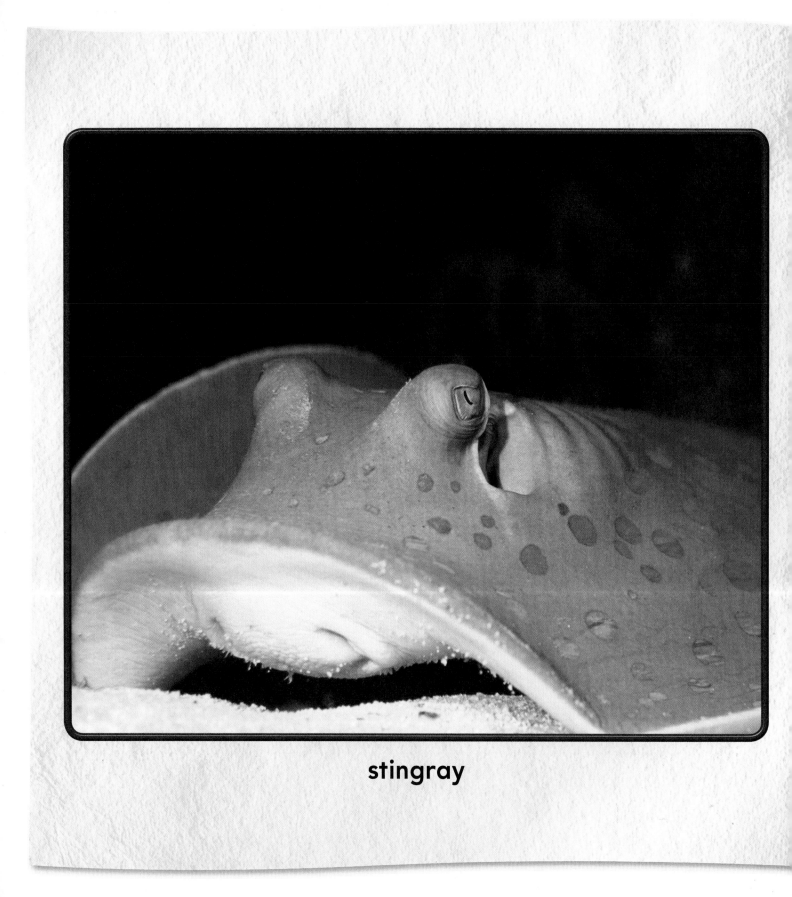

stingray

This flat fish has big blue spots.

ghost pipefish

This thin fish has pink spots.

sea slug

Some animals must be in water
to live. This sea slug can rest
on rocks in the water.

crab

Some animals can live in water and on land. This crab can run and dig in the sand.

penguins

Penguins can live where it is cold.
They just had a cold swim. Brrr!

California sea lions

Sea lions can live where it is warm.
They will nap on rocks in the sun.

A turtle is not fast on land.
It can swim fast in water.

It has flippers that help it swim fast. It can swim far.

sea star

Sea stars are not fast. They take little steps on sand and rocks.

moray eels

Some animals eat plants. Lots of them eat fish. Some will hunt for a snack with a pal.

The sea is full of lots of animals.
The water is their home.

1. How do captions help you learn in this story?

⬭ They tell where sea animals live.

⬭ They tell the names of sea animals.

⬭ They tell how to find sea animals.

TEKS 1.14D

2. ✔ **TARGET SKILL** **Author's Purpose**

Why was this story mainly written?
TEKS 1.13; **ELPS** 4J

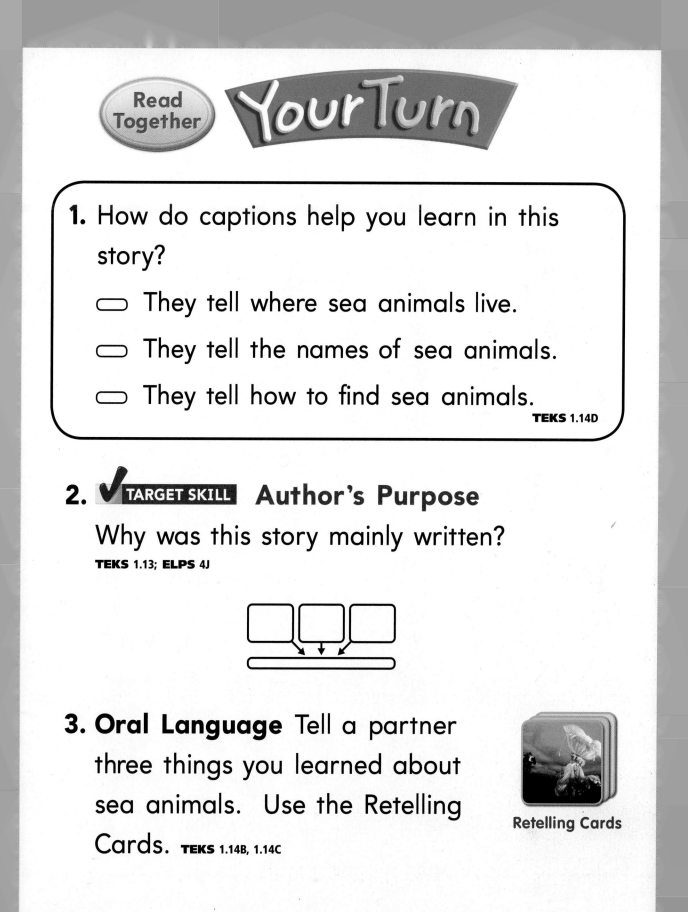

3. **Oral Language** Tell a partner three things you learned about sea animals. Use the Retelling Cards. **TEKS** 1.14B, 1.14C

Retelling Cards

TEKS **1.13** identify topic/explain author's purpose; **1.14B** identify important facts/details; **1.14C** retell order of events; **1.14D** use text features to locate information; **ELPS 4J** employ inferential skills to demonstrate comprehension

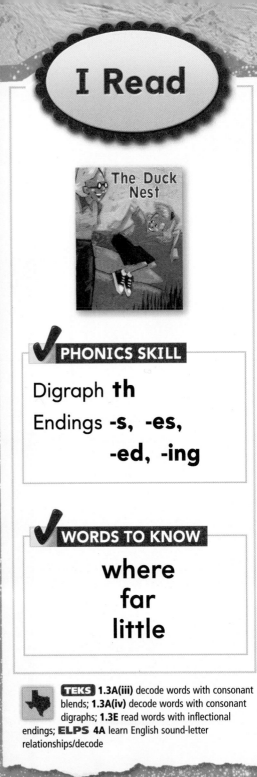

The Duck Nest

✔ **PHONICS SKILL**

Digraph **th**
Endings **-s, -es,
-ed, -ing**

✔ **WORDS TO KNOW**

**where
far
little**

TEKS **1.3A(iii)** decode words with consonant blends; **1.3A(iv)** decode words with consonant digraphs; **1.3E** read words with inflectional endings; **ELPS** **4A** learn English sound-letter relationships/decode

The Duck Nest

by Michael Frost
illustrated by Joe Cepeda

Beth Ann was with Gram.

Beth Ann jumped and jumped.

Then Beth Ann quit jumping!

"Is that a nest?" Beth Ann
asked Gram.
"Yes," said Gram. "It is a
duck nest filled with eggs."

"Gram, is that egg cracked?"
asked Beth Ann.
"Yes," said Gram. "That egg
has lots of cracks."

"Look at this little duck!" said
Gram.
"Where is its mom?" Beth Ann
asked. "I bet it misses its mom."

"Not far," said Gram. "That big duck must be its mom. She will not come back with us here." Gram and Beth Ann left.

Mom Duck did not see Beth Ann and Gram. She went back to the nest. Mom Duck had a bug.

Did that little duck get that bug?
Yes! Yum! Yum!

Water

Connect to Science

✓ **WORDS TO KNOW**

cold   far
where   their
blue   little
live   water

GENRE

Informational text gives facts about a topic. This is from a science textbook.

TEXT FOCUS

Illustrations are pictures that show more about the text.

TEKS 1.3H identify/read high-frequency words; **ELPS** 4F use visual/contextual/peer/ teacher support to read/comprehend texts

Water

What is one thing that all living things, whether they are big or little, have in common? They need water to live.

Water comes in different forms. The water you drink is a liquid. A liquid flows and takes the shape of the container it is in.

ice

water

snow

Water can freeze into ice or snow. Frozen water is a solid. A solid has its own shape.

What is ice? Ice is water that has frozen. It is hard and cold.

Where does snow come from? Snow is tiny pieces of frozen water that fall from the clouds.

Ice and snow are found in many places around the world. The North Pole is one of these places. There is cold, blue water all around it. People cannot live that far north for very long, but some animals make their homes near the North Pole.

Making Connections

Read Together

Text to Self
TEKS 1.19C, 1.20A(iii), RC-1(F)

Write to Describe Think about your favorite sea animal from the selection. Write sentences to describe it to a classmate.

Text to Text
TEKS 1.14D, RC-1(F)

Connect to Science Look at the pictures in **Sea Animals**. How many forms of water do you see? What are they?

Text to World
TEKS 1.20A(ii), 1.24A, RC-1(F)

Use a Globe Use a globe to find two different oceans. Draw and label sea animals that you think might live in each ocean.

TEKS **1.14D** use text features to locate information; **1.19C** write brief comments on texts; **1.20A(ii)** understand/use nouns; **1.20A(iii)** understand/use adjectives; **1.24A** gather evidence; **RC-1(F)** make connections to experiences/texts/community; **ELPS 1E** internalize new basic/academic language; **3D** speak using content area vocabulary

43

TEKS 1.6A identify nouns/verbs; 1.20A(ii) understand/use nouns; 1.21B(iii) capitalize names of people; ELPS 1E internalize new basic/ academic language; 5E employ increasingly complex grammatical structures in writing

Grammar

Proper Nouns A noun that names a special person or animal is called a **proper noun**. Proper nouns begin with capital letters.

When a **title** is used before a name, it begins with a capital letter, too. A title usually ends with a period.

Mr. Diaz   **Mrs.** Sims   **Miss Reed**

Make up a name for each person and animal and write it on another sheet of paper. Use at least one title. Share your names with classmates.

1.

2.

3.

4.

5.

Grammar in Writing

When you proofread your writing, be sure you have written the names of people and animals correctly.

TEKS 1.17D edit drafts; 1.20A(iv) understand/use adverbs; ELPS 5C spell English words with increasing accuracy; 5G narrate/describe/explain in writing

Write to Inform

Read Together

✔ **Sentence Fluency** Sometimes you will write **sentences** that give readers facts. One kind of fact describes how something happens.

Joy wrote about sea lions. Then she added **loudly** to describe how sea lions bark.

Revised Draft

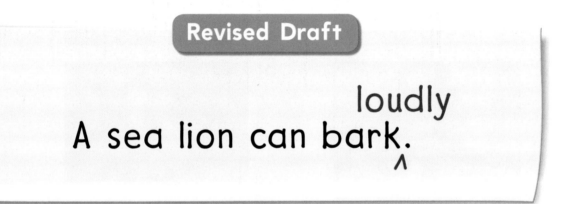

A sea lion can bark. loudly

Writing Traits Checklist

✔ **Sentence Fluency** Do my sentences have words that tell **how**?

 Did I spell words correctly?

 Did I use capital letters correctly?

Look for words that tell **how** in Joy's final copy. Then revise your writing. Use the Checklist.

Sea Lions

Sea lions do amazing things. A sea lion can bark loudly. It uses its flippers to move quickly on land or in water.

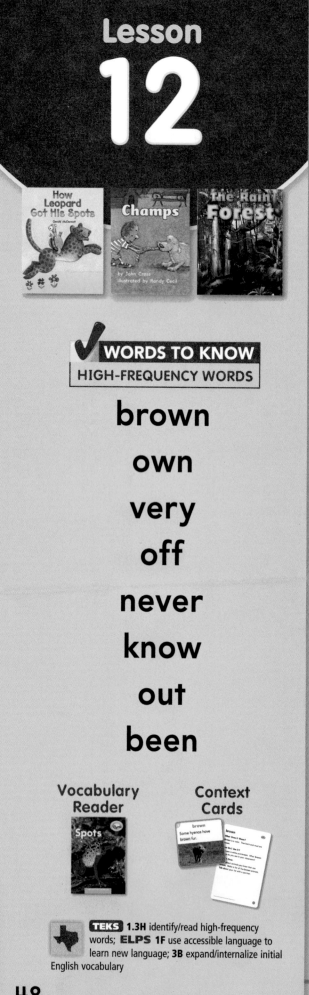

✓ **WORDS TO KNOW**
HIGH-FREQUENCY WORDS

brown

own

very

off

never

know

out

been

Vocabulary
Reader

Spots

Context
Cards

TEKS 1.3H identify/read high-frequency
words; **ELPS** 1F use accessible language to
learn new language; 3B expand/internalize initial
English vocabulary

48

Words to Know

● **Read** each Context Card.

● **Describe** a picture, using the blue word.

1

brown

Some hyenas have brown fur.

2

own

Zebras know their own mother by her stripes.

3 very
The snake in that tree is very long.

4 off
The bird flew off the rock and into the air.

5 never
Rhinos eat plants.
They never eat meat.

6 know
Leopards know how to climb trees.

7 out
The turtle climbed out of the pond.

8 been
The giraffes have been moving fast.

TEKS 1.3H identify/read high-frequency words; **1.6D** categorize words; **RC-1(F)** make connections to experiences/tetxs/community; **ELPS** 4D use prereading supports to comprehend texts; **4F** use visual/contextual/peer/teacher support to read/comprehend texts

Background

Read Together

✓ **WORDS TO KNOW** Animals with Spots

1. You never know which spotted animals you might see when you go out.

2. There have been cows with very big spots.

3. Baby deer are brown with white spots.

4. Look at a ladybug's spots before it flies off.

5. Make your own list of animals with spots.

Some Animals with Spots

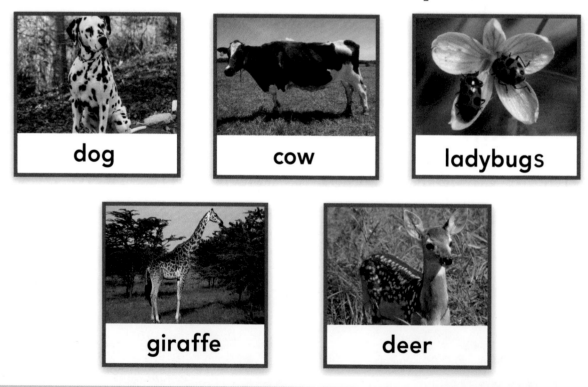

dog

cow

ladybugs

giraffe

deer

Comprehension

Read Together

✓ **TARGET SKILL** Sequence of Events

Most story events are told in time order. This order is called the **sequence of events**. Good readers think about what happens **first, next,** and **last** so that a story makes sense. Tell about the sequence of events in this leopard's life.

As you read **How Leopard Got His Spots**, think about the sequence of events.

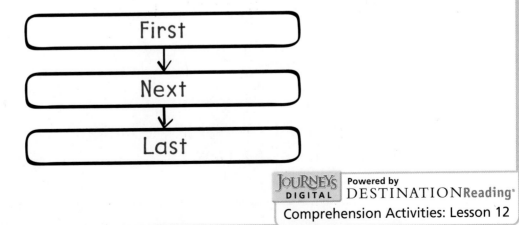

First

↓

Next

↓

Last

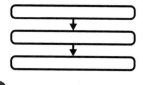

✔ WORDS TO KNOW

brown	never
own	know
very	out
off	been

✔ TARGET SKILL

Sequence of Events
Tell the order in which things happen.

✔ TARGET STRATEGY

Question Ask questions about the story.

GENRE

A **folktale** is an old story people tell. Why is **once upon a time** used in this folktale?

TEKS **1.4B** ask questions/seek clarification/ locate details about texts; **1.7B** understand recurring phrases in traditional tales; **1.27A** listen attentively/ask relevant questions; **RC-1(B)** ask literal questions of text

Meet the Author and Illustrator

Gerald McDermott

When he was just four years old, Gerald McDermott started taking art lessons at a museum. Saturdays were spent at the museum drawing, painting, and looking at the artwork. Mr. McDermott's book **Arrow to the Sun** won the Caldecott Medal for best illustrations.

How Leopard Got His Spots

written and illustrated by Gerald McDermott

Essential Question

Why is the order of story events important?

Do you know how
Leopard got his spots?

Once upon a time, Fred
Turtle was playing catch with
Hal Hyena. Hal tricked Fred.
Then he ran away.

Fred felt very sad.
He called out for help.
"Help! I am stuck in
the plants," he yelled.

Len Leopard ran to help.

Chop! Chop! Chop!
Len cut the plants off and
let Fred out.

Fred and Len danced in
the sun.
"This is such fun!" they said.

"I have never been this glad,"
said Fred. "I like to paint if I
am glad!"

Fred mixed paints from many flowers. Then he painted black stripes on Zel Zebra.

Fred painted Jill Giraffe next.
"Look at me!" said Jill.
"I have big brown spots now."

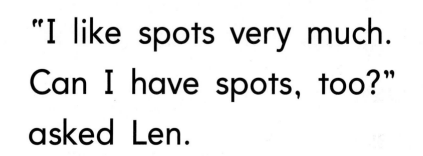

"I like spots very much.
Can I have spots, too?"
asked Len.

Fred got set to paint Len.

Now Len had spots
of his very own.

Zel, Jill, and Len had such
fun looking at their spots
and stripes.
Hal said, "Paint me, too!"

But Fred had a trick for Hal.
He splashed Hal with brown
paint. Hal yelled and ran off.

Now Fred and Len
are best friends.

Read Together

Your Turn

1. In the story, the word <u>never</u> means —

◯ always

◯ not ever

◯ just once

TEKS 1.6C

2. ✔ TARGET SKILL **Sequence of Events**
What happens after Len cuts the plants off
of Fred? TEKS 1.9A, RC-1(E); ELPS 4I

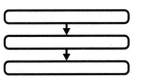

3. Oral Language Use the Retelling
Cards to act out the story with
four classmates. Decide who will
be each character. TEKS 1.9A, RC-1(E)

Retelling Cards

TEKS **1.6C** use syntax/context to determine meaning; **1.9A** retell story events; **RC-1(E)** retell/act out important story events;
ELPS 4I employ reading skills to demonstrate comprehension

Champs

by John Cross
illustrated by Randy Cecil

I Read

Champs

by John Cross
illustrated by Randy Cecil

✔ **PHONICS SKILL**

Digraphs **ch, tch**
Possessives with **'s**

✔ **WORDS TO KNOW**

own
know
been

TEKS **1.3A(i)** decode words with consonants; **1.3A(ii)** decode words with vowels; **1.3A(iv)** decode words with consonant digraphs; **1.3H** identify/read high-frequency words; **ELPS** **4A** learn English sound-letter relationships/decode

Dutch is Bill's dog.
Dutch and Bill play tug.
Dutch is the tug champ.

Bill sits on his bench to rest.

Dutch has his own spot to rest.

Dutch's spot is not a bench.

Fran is here. Fran is Bill's pal.
Chet is Fran's dog. Dutch and
Chet play. Bill and Fran chat.

Dutch and Chet like to play with
Bill and Fran. Dutch and Chet get
set to play catch. They know Bill
and Fran will play with them.

"Catch it, Dutch!" yells Bill.
Dutch jumps up, up, up to catch.
Then Fran yells, "Catch it, Chet!"
Chet jumps and catches, too.

It has been such fun! Fran pets
Chet, and Bill pets Dutch.

Chet and Dutch are such good dogs! They are champs!

Connect to Science

✔ **WORDS TO KNOW**

brown	never
own	know
very	out
off	been

GENRE

Informational text gives facts about a topic. This is from a science textbook.

TEXT FOCUS

A **map** is a drawing of a town, state, or other place.

TEKS 1.3H identify/read high-frequency words; **ELPS** 4F use visual/contextual/peer/ teacher support to read/comprehend texts

The Rain Forest

A rain forest is a very wet and warm place. Rain forests have layers. Each layer has its own animals that live in it.

Canopy Layer The tops of trees poking out above the forest form this layer. The tree leaves and branches keep most sunlight off the layers below. Eagles, sloths, and monkeys live here.

Understory Layer This layer is above the ground. It is shady. Young trees and bushes grow here. Frogs, birds, and snakes live here.

79

Forest Floor Sunlight almost never reaches this layer. Tapirs, jaguars, and beetles live on the brown forest floor. Ants and giant anteaters also live there. Anteaters have been known to eat thirty thousand insects in a single day!

NORTH AMERICA

EUROPE

ASIA

AFRICA

Equator

SOUTH AMERICA

AUSTRALIA

Map Key

Rain forest

ANTARCTICA

Do you know where the world's rain forests are? This map shows you.

Making Connections

hugeRead Together

Text to Self

TEKS 1.7B, 1.18A, RC-1(F)

Write a Story What does **once upon a time** mean? Write a story about an animal you might see near your home. Begin your story with **once upon a time**.

Text to Text

TEKS 1.4B, 1.14B, RC-1(F)

Connect to Science Look back at both selections. Tell how the places where the animals live are alike and different. Talk about the clues in the text that help you know.

Text to World

TEKS 1.15B, 1.24C, RC-1(F)

Make a Map Pretend that you are in a rain forest. Draw a map showing where you will go. Explain any symbols you use.

 TEKS 1.4B ask questions/seek clarification/locate details about texts; **1.7B** understand recurring phrases in traditional tales; **1.14B** identify important facts/details; **1.15B** explain signs/symbols; **1.18A** write brief stories; **1.24C** record information in visual formats; **RC-1(F)** make connection to experiences/texts/community; **ELPS 5B** write using new basic/content-based vocabulary

81

Grammar

Proper Nouns A noun that names a special place is also a **proper noun**. Proper nouns begin with capital letters.

Write each sentence correctly. Use another sheet of paper.

1. I go to the pratt school.

2. My class took a trip to the kent zoo.

3. It is on ash street in hampton.

4. Next year I am moving to texas.

5. My new house is near fisher lake.

Grammar in Writing

When you proofread your writing, be sure you have written the names of places correctly.

TEKS **1.15A** follow written multi-step directions; **1.17C** revise drafts; **1.17D** edit drafts; **1.19B** write short letters; **1.20A(vii)** understand/use time-order transition words; **ELPS 5D** edit writing for standard grammar/usage; **5F** use a variety of sentence types in writing; **5G** narrate/describe/explain in writing

Write to Inform  Read Together

✔ **Sentence Fluency** In good **instructions**, the sentences tell the steps in order. Order words help make the steps easy to follow.

Akil drafted his instructions in a letter to his friend Pam. Later, he added the order word **Last**.

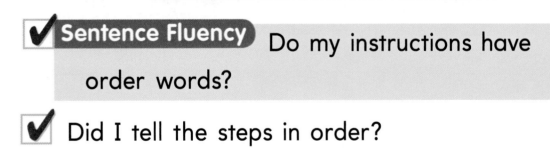

Revised Draft

Last,
4. ̸Color brown spots.
  ^

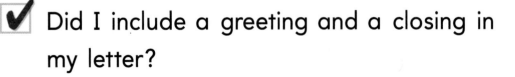

Writing Traits Checklist

✔ **Sentence Fluency** Do my instructions have order words?

✔ Did I tell the steps in order?

✔ Did I include a greeting and a closing in my letter?

84

Revise your work using the Checklist.
Follow Akil's instructions to make a puppet!

Final Copy

Dear Pam,

I made a leopard puppet. Here is
how you can make one, too.

1. First, get a small paper bag.
2. Next, fold the sides of the flap.
3. Then, glue on ears, eyes, a nose,
   and whiskers.
4. Last, color brown spots.

I hope you have fun making
your puppet.

        Your friend,

        Akil

Lesson 13

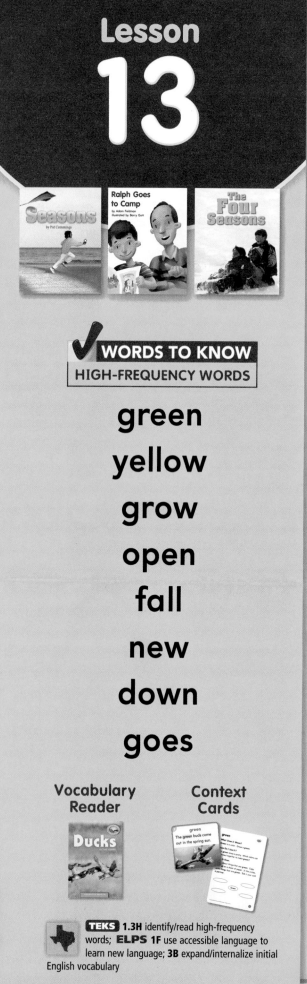

✓ **WORDS TO KNOW**
HIGH-FREQUENCY WORDS

green
yellow
grow
open
fall
new
down
goes

Vocabulary
Reader

Context
Cards

TEKS 1.3H identify/read high-frequency words; **ELPS 1F** use accessible language to learn new language; **3B** expand/internalize initial English vocabulary

86

Words to Know

Read Together

● Read each Context Card.

● Choose two blue words.
Use them in sentences.

1
green
The green buds come out in the spring sun.

2
yellow
He put on yellow boots on a rainy day.

3 grow

Many flowers grow in the summer.

4 open

The windows can be open on a hot day.

5 fall

The leaves change color in fall.

6 new

She has a brand new backpack for school.

7 down

Snow comes down on a cold day.

8 goes

She goes to the park to skate with her mom.

TEKS 1.3H identify/read high-frequency words; **RC-1(F)** make connections to experiences/texts/community; **ELPS 4D** use prereading supports to comprehend texts; **4F** use visual/contextual/peer/teacher support to read/comprehend texts

Background

✓ WORDS TO KNOW **Four Seasons**

1. Winter comes and goes.

2. A new season starts. It is spring!

3. Green plants grow. Then it is summer.

4. Many flowers are open in summer.

5. Fall comes next. Leaves turn yellow.

6. Snow falls down. Winter is here again.

Spring

Summer

Fall

Winter

Comprehension

✓ **TARGET SKILL** Cause and Effect

One story event can make, or cause, another event to happen. The **cause** happens first. It is the reason why something else happens. The **effect** is what happens because of the first event.

Cause: It is raining.
Effect: The girls stand under an umbrella.

As you read **Seasons**, think about what happens in each season and why.

What happens?	Why?

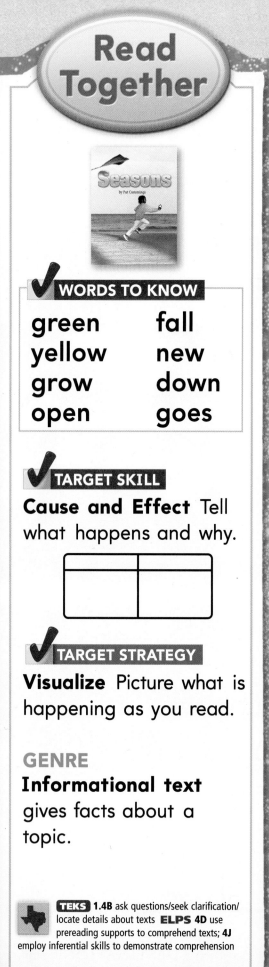

Read Together

Seasons
by Pat Cummings

✔ WORDS TO KNOW

green	fall
yellow	new
grow	down
open	goes

✔ TARGET SKILL

Cause and Effect Tell what happens and why.

✔ TARGET STRATEGY

Visualize Picture what is happening as you read.

GENRE

Informational text gives facts about a topic.

TEKS 1.4B ask questions/seek clarification/ locate details about texts **ELPS** 4D use prereading supports to comprehend texts; 4J employ inferential skills to demonstrate comprehension

Meet the Author

Pat Cummings

Pat Cummings loves getting letters from kids who have read her books. Sometimes they send her other things too, such as T-shirts, mugs, drawings, and even science projects. **Clean Your Room, Harvey Moon!** is just one of her many books.

Seasons

written by Pat Cummings

Essential Question

What changes do the different seasons cause?

Spring

In the spring,
fresh winds blow.
We plant new seeds,
and green buds grow.

Eggs hatch open.
Little chicks sing.
The sun is out.
It must be spring!

The grass gets wet.
Splish! Splash! Splish!
When we step,
we hear it squish.

Summer

Then summer is here
and it gets hot.
We are not in school.
We play a lot.

Bugs buzz and hum.
The plants grow tall.
Next to them,
I look small.

Summer goes fast,
and when it ends,
we will go back to school!
with all our friends.

Fall

In fall the leaves
are red, yellow, and brown.
In a gust of wind,
they will fall down.

The leaves crunch
as we jump and hop.
It is such fun,
we cannot stop!

Animals get nuts
and pack them away.
They will have lots to eat
on a cold day.

Winter

When it is winter,
cold winds blow.
It is fun to sled
on the soft snow.

When it is cold,
some animals rest.
This animal has
a nap in a nest.

A hat on a shelf
gives us a plan.
We will put the hat
on a big snowman!

Winter

 **Spring**

 **Summer**

 **Fall**

Winter, Spring,
Summer, Fall.
Which is best?
We like them all!

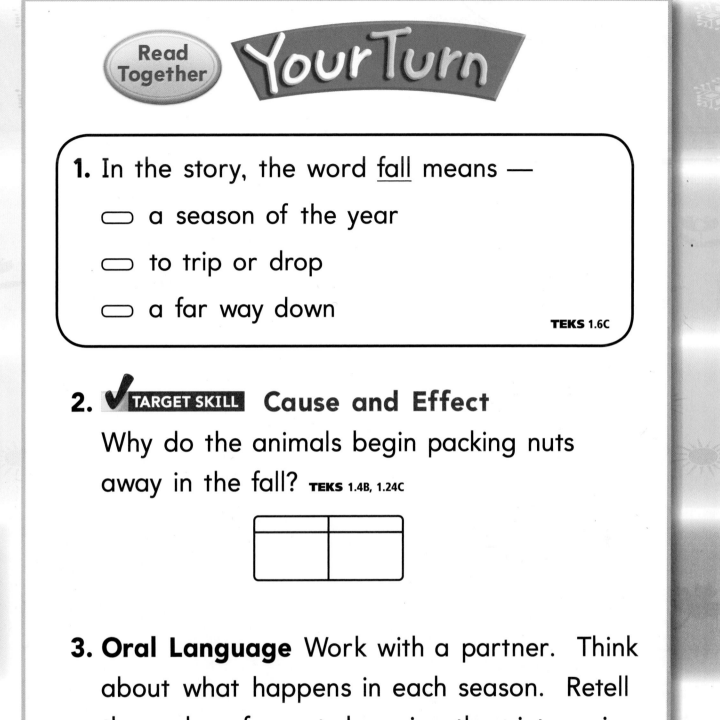

Read Together Your Turn

1. In the story, the word <u>fall</u> means —

⬭ a season of the year

⬭ to trip or drop

⬭ a far way down

TEKS 1.6C

2. ✔ TARGET SKILL **Cause and Effect**

Why do the animals begin packing nuts away in the fall? TEKS 1.4B, 1.24C

3. Oral Language Work with a partner. Think about what happens in each season. Retell the order of events by using the pictures in the story. Take turns telling something you like to do in each season. TEKS 1.14B, 1.14C, RC-1(F)

TEKS 1.4B ask questions/seek clarification/locate details about texts; 1.6C use syntax/context to determine meaning; 1.14B identify important facts/details; 1.14C retell order of events; 1.24C record information in visual formats; RC-1(F) make connections to experiences/ texts/community; **ELPS** 4I employ reading skills to demonstrate comprehension

I Read

Ralph Goes to Camp
by Adam Feldman
illustrated by Barry Gott

✔ PHONICS SKILL

Digraphs **sh, wh, ph**
Contractions **'s, n't**

✔ WORDS TO KNOW

goes
yellow

TEKS 1.3A(i) decode words with consonants; 1.3A(ii) decode words with vowels; 1.3A(iv) decode words with consonant digraphs; 1.3G identify/read contractions; 1.3H identify/read high-frequency words

Ralph Goes to Camp

by Adam Feldman

illustrated by Barry Gott

Ralph asks his mom and dad if he can go to camp.

"Yes," said Dad, "if you do some jobs."

Ralph was shocked.
"Jobs?" Ralph asked.

"Yes," said Dad, "but it isn't that bad.
It's just the dog and the trash."

Shep is Ralph's dog. Ralph had to give Shep a bath. Shep had fun splishing and splashing. Ralph got wet, but Ralph did his job well.

When Ralph had to tug big trash
bins, he didn't rush. Ralph didn't
spill trash. Ralph didn't trip.
Ralph did his job well.

"Ralph goes to camp today!" said
Ralph's mom.
Ralph got his yellow bag and hat.

Ralph went to camp at last!
Ralph had fun at camp, and he
had no jobs!

Connect to Poetry

✔ **WORDS TO KNOW**

green	fall
yellow	new
grow	down
open	goes

GENRE

Poetry uses the sound of words to show pictures and feelings. Listen for rhythm and rhyme in the following poems.

TEXT FOCUS

Onomatopoeia is the use of words that imitate sounds.

TEKS **1.3H** identify/read high-frequency words; **1.8** respond to/use rhythm/rhyme/alliteration; **ELPS** **2A** distinguish sounds/intonation patterns of English; **4D** use prereading supports to comprehend texts

The Four Seasons

The year goes by fast. Each season brings many changes. We see green grass grow each summer. In the fall, red and yellow leaves drift down from the trees. Snow comes in winter, and new flowers open up in spring.

Spring Song

The winter snow melts away
and the air is soft this sunny day.
What does this gentle wind sing?
I know! I know!
Here comes Spring!

by Charlotte Zolotow

Listen

Scrunch, scrunch, scrunch.
Crunch, crunch, crunch.
Frozen snow and brittle ice
Make a winter sound that's nice
Underneath my stamping feet
And the cars along the street.
Scrunch, scrunch, scrunch.
Crunch, crunch, crunch.

by Margaret Hillert

Seasons Song

to the tune of "Twinkle, Twinkle, Little Star"

Winter, spring, summer, fall,
Which one is the best of all?
Winter has the cold and snow.
Spring has rain so flowers grow.
Summer has the hot, hot sun.
Fall has school and friends and fun.

Write About the Seasons

Draw a picture of your favorite season. Then write a poem about it. Try using rhyming words and sound words.

Making Connections

Text to Self

TEKS 1.19C, 1.20A(iii), RC-1(F)

Write to Describe What is your favorite season? Write sentences to describe it.

Text to Text

TEKS 1.8, RC-1(F)

Connect to Poetry List pairs of rhyming words from the selections. Choose a pair and write two more rhyming words.

Text to World

TEKS RC-1(F)

Tell About Seasons Locate Texas on a globe. Then locate a country. Tell how you think seasons in both places might be the same or different.

 TEKS 1.8 respond to/use rhythm/rhyme/alliteration; **1.19C** write brief comments on texts; **1.20A(iii)** understand/use adjectives; **RC-1(F)** make connections to experiences/texts/community; **ELPS** **1E** internalize new basic/academic language; **2E** use support to enhance/confirm understanding of spoken language; **3J** respond orally to information in media

TEKS **1.6A** identify nouns/verbs; **1.20A(i)** understand/use verbs; **1.20B** speak in complete sentences **ELPS 5D** edit writing for standard grammar/usage; **5E** employ increasingly complex grammatical structures in writing

Grammar

Subjects and Verbs In a sentence, the subject and the verb have to agree. Both must tell about the same number of people or things. Add **s** to most **verbs** when they tell about a **noun** that names one.

One	More Than One
One **boy** pull**s** his sled.	Two **girls** pull their dog.
Brett slide**s** down the hill.	**Children** slide across the pond.

Choose the correct verb to finish each sentence. Take turns reading a sentence aloud with a partner. Then talk about how you chose the correct verb.

1. Raindrops _____?_____ each spring.
   fall   falls

2. Flowers _____?_____ in the garden.
   grow   grows

3. One bug _____?_____ all night.
   hum   hums

4. Now the sun _____?_____ brightly.
   shine   shines

5. The children _____?_____ in the pool.
   swim   swims

Grammar in Writing

When you proofread your writing, be sure you have written the correct verb to go with each noun.

Write to Inform

Read Together

✔️ **Ideas**   When you write **sentences** that tell facts, be sure all your sentences are about one main idea.

Kyle wrote about winter. Then he took out a sentence that didn't belong.

Revised Draft

Winter is the coldest season.

Sometimes it snows here.

~~I have a dog.~~

Writing Traits Checklist

✔️ **Ideas**   Are all my sentences about one main idea? I will delete the sentences that are not.

✔️ Does each detail sentence tell a fact?

✔️ Did I write the correct verb to go with each noun?

Look for the main idea sentence in Kyle's final copy. Then revise your writing. Use the Checklist.

Final Copy

A Chilly Season

Winter is the coldest season.

Sometimes it snows here.

The lake freezes.

People skate on it.

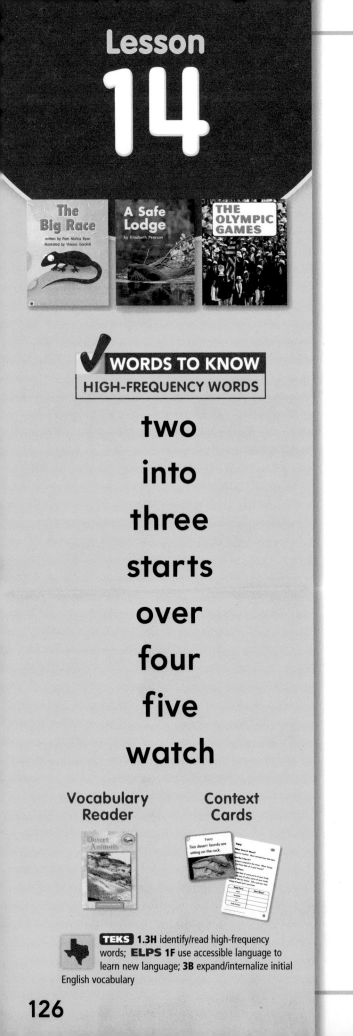

The Big Race
written by Pam Muñoz Ryan
illustrated by Viviana Garofoli

A Safe Lodge
by Elizabeth Pearson

THE OLYMPIC GAMES

✔ WORDS TO KNOW
HIGH-FREQUENCY WORDS

two
into
three
starts
over
four
five
watch

Vocabulary Reader

Context Cards

TEKS 1.3H identify/read high-frequency words; ELPS 1F use accessible language to learn new language; 3B expand/internalize initial English vocabulary

126

Words to Know

- Read each Context Card.
- Use a blue word to tell about something you did.

1

two

Two desert lizards are sitting on the rock.

2

into

The bird flew into the big cactus.

3 **three**

There are three birds resting in the sun.

4 **starts**

The desert starts to cool down at sunset.

5 **over**

A hawk flew over the tall rocks.

6 **four**

All four legs of this fox are strong.

7 **five**

This desert flower has five red spots.

8 **watch**

The rabbits watch and listen for danger.

Background

✔ **WORDS TO KNOW** **Running Contest**

1. The race starts at four o'clock.

2. We watch the runners get into place.

3. Five runners start to go fast.

4. Then three of the runners slow down.

5. Two runners are very close.

6. The winner goes over the finish line!

Who do you think will win this race?
Tell about races you have been in.

TEKS 1.4C establish purpose/monitor comprehension; **RC-1(A)** establish reading purposes; **RC-1(D)** make inferences/use textual evidence; **ELPS 1E** internalize new basic/academic language; **4D** use prereading supports to comprehend texts; **4F** use visual/contextual/peer/teacher support to read/comprehend texts

Comprehension

Read Together

✔ **TARGET SKILL** Conclusions

In a story, authors do not always tell all the details. Readers must use story clues and what they already know to make a smart guess about what the author does not say. This smart guess is a **conclusion**.

Conclusion: The boy won.
What clues helped you know this?

As you read **The Big Race**, use story clues and what you already know to think of conclusions. Use a chart like this one to tell what helps Red Lizard win the race.

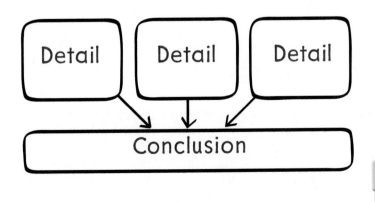

JOURNEYS DIGITAL **Powered by** DESTINATIONReading®
Comprehension Activities: Lesson 14

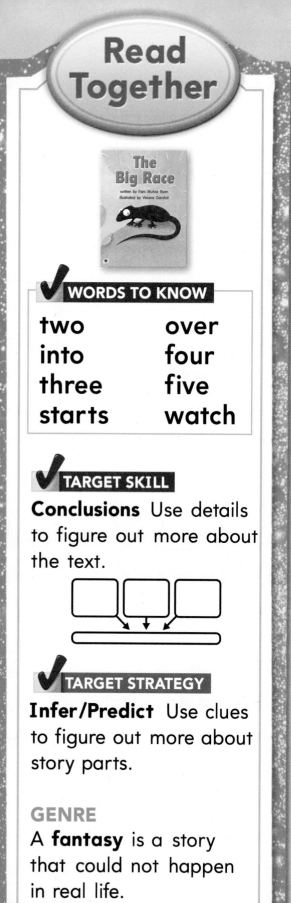

The
Big Race

written by Pam Muñoz Ryan
illustrated by Viviana Garofoli

✔ WORDS TO KNOW

two	over
into	four
three	five
starts	watch

✔ TARGET SKILL

Conclusions Use details to figure out more about the text.

✔ TARGET STRATEGY

Infer/Predict Use clues to figure out more about story parts.

GENRE

A **fantasy** is a story that could not happen in real life.

TEKS 1.4B ask questions/seek clarification/locate details about texts; **RC-1(D)** make inferences/use textual evidence; **ELPS 4J** employ inferential skills to demonstrate comprehension

Meet the Author

Pam Muñoz Ryan

California summers can be very hot. When Pam Muñoz Ryan was growing up, she was often at the library on summer days. That's because the library was one of the few places nearby with air conditioning!

Meet the Illustrator

Viviana Garofoli

Viviana Garofoli and her family make their home in the country of Argentina. **Sophie's Trophy** and **My Big Rig** are two of the books she has illustrated.

The Big Race

written by Pam Muñoz Ryan

illustrated by Viviana Garofoli

Essential Question

What clues help you figure out why events happen?

Win the Big Race
Win this Big Cake

Today is the big race.

"I like cake!" said Red Lizard.
"I will run in that race."

Red Lizard gets to the race.
Four animals will run with him.

Cottontail is not late.
She will run in lane one.

Rat naps in the shade.
She will run in lane two.

Snake takes his spot in lane three.

Roadrunner stands in lane four.

He waves to his pals.

Red Lizard is in lane five.
The animals bend and hop.

The flag is down, and the race starts!
Many animals watch and clap.

Cottontail does not get far.

Rat falls into the hay.

Snake stops and chases bugs.

Roadrunner trips over a rake.

Who will win?

It's Red Lizard who wins!

"Watch me eat this cake," he yells.
Red Lizard looks at his big cake.

Red Lizard looks at his pals.

His pals like cake, too.
What will Red Lizard do now?

Red Lizard gets five plates.
He gets cake for his pals, too.
Hip, Hip, Hooray for Red Lizard!

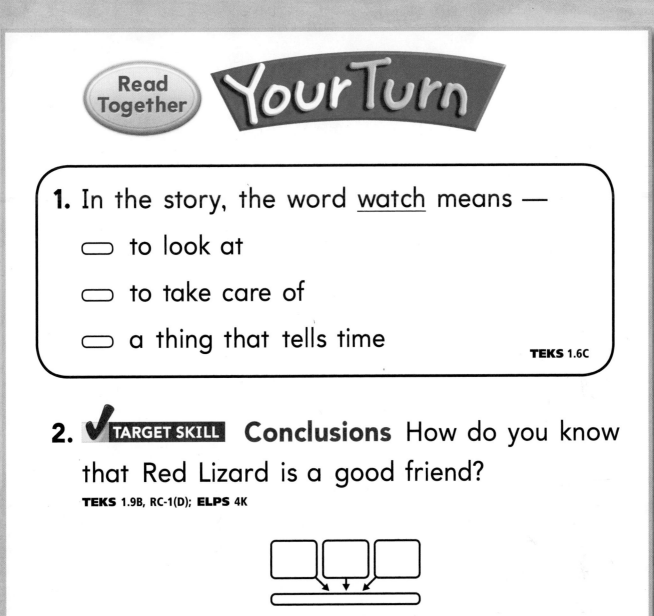

Read Together — Your Turn

1. In the story, the word <u>watch</u> means —

⬭ to look at

⬭ to take care of

⬭ a thing that tells time

TEKS 1.6C

2. ✔ **TARGET SKILL** **Conclusions** How do you know that Red Lizard is a good friend?

TEKS 1.9B, RC-1(D); **ELPS** 4K

3. Oral Language Work with a partner. Speak clearly as you tell about your favorite part of the story. Use the Retelling Cards to help you. **TEKS** 1.9A, 1.28

Retelling Cards

 TEKS **1.6C** use syntax/context to determine meaning; **1.9A** retell story events; **1.9B** describe/analyze characters; **1.28** share information/ideas by speaking clearly; **RC–1(D)** make inferences/use textual evidence; **ELPS 4K** employ analytical skills to demonstrate comprehension

A Safe Lodge
by Elizabeth Pearson

TEKS **1.3A(i)** decode words with consonants; **1.3A(ii)** decode words with vowels; **1.3C(iv)** decode using VCe pattern; **ELPS 4C** develop/comprehend basic English vocabulary and structures

A Safe Lodge

by Elizabeth Pearson

This is an animal that can make its own lodge. It starts with sticks.

This animal cuts sticks. It drags the
sticks and makes a big lodge with them.

This lodge is a safe place. It is in a lake. It is made of sticks and mud.

This lodge has space for kits.
Kits romp and rest. When kits get
big, they can go out. They can
watch Dad and Mom cut sticks.

Big kits can cut sticks. Kits can
drag sticks and help make a dam.
A dam holds water back.

Mom, Dad, and the kits made this
dam. If water spills over it, Mom,
Dad, and the kits will fix it.

This dam helps make the lodge safe.

Connect to Social Studies

✔ **WORDS TO KNOW**

two	over
into	four
three	five
starts	watch

GENRE

Informational text gives facts about a topic. This is a magazine article.

TEXT FOCUS

Captions tell more information about a photo or picture. Read captions to find facts.

TEKS 1.3H identify/read high-frequency words; **1.14B** identify important facts and details; **1.14D** use text features to locate information; **ELPS 4F** use visual/contextual/peer/teacher support to read/comprehend texts

THE OLYMPIC GAMES

by Margaret Bishop

The Olympic Games are sports games. Athletes come from many countries to play. Many people watch, too. Here are three American athletes who have been in the Olympics.

A parade starts the Olympic Games.

Lake Placid, New York, 1980

Eric Heiden was a speed skater. He was in five races, and he won all of them! He skated into history.

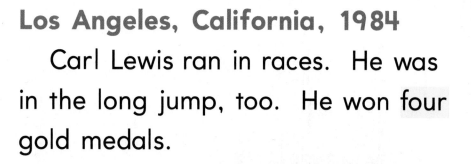

Los Angeles, California, 1984

Carl Lewis ran in races. He was in the long jump, too. He won four gold medals.

Carl won nine gold medals in four different Olympics.

FROM THE PAGES OF
WEEKLY READER

WR™

Atlanta, Georgia, 1996

Kerri Strug had two tries to go over the vault. She fell once, but she tried again. She did it!

Making Connections

Text to Self

TEKS 1.21B(i); RC-1(F)

Write About Sports Which sport would you like to win? Draw yourself winning. Write a sentence to go with it. Capitalize the first word.

Text to Text

TEKS 1.10; 1.29; RC-1(F)

Connect to Social Studies Discuss with a partner which selection is real and which is fantasy. Take turns and tell what text clues help you know.

Text to World

TEKS 1.15B; RC1(F)

Map a Race Course Pretend you will run a race through your neighborhood. Where does the race begin? Where is the finish line? Draw a race course map.

 TEKS 1.10 distinguish true stories from fantasies; **1.15B** explain signs/symbols; **1.21B(i)** capitalize beginning of sentences; **1.27A** listen attentively/ask relevant questions; **1.29** follow discussion rules; **RC-1(F)** make connections to experiences/texts/community; **ELPS 1C** use strategic learning techniques; **2E** use support to enhance/confirm understanding of spoken language

Grammar

Verbs and Time **Verbs** can name actions. Some verbs tell what actions are happening now. Some verbs tell what actions happened in the past. Add **ed** to most verbs to tell about the past.

Now	In the Past
The **animals watch** the race now.	The **animals watched** the race yesterday.
They cheer for their friends.	**They cheered** for their friends.

Work with a partner. One partner reads aloud a sentence. The other partner identifies the word that names an action. Together, tell how to write the verb to tell about the past. Take turns.

1. The runners look at the flag.

2. They start the race.

3. Some racers jump high.

4. They finish the race quickly.

5. The winners pick prizes.

Grammar in Writing

When you proofread your writing, be sure each verb tells clearly if something is happening now or in the past.

TEKS 1.17A generate ideas for writing; **1.23A** generate topics/formulate questions: **1.23B** determine relevant sources of information; **1.24A** gather evidence; **1.24C** record information in visual formats; **ELPS 5G** narrate/describe /explain in writing

Reading-Writing Workshop: Prewrite

Write to Inform (Read Together)

☑ **Ideas**   A good **report** needs facts!
Before you start writing, find facts to answer
the question you wrote about your topic.
   Lena found information about lizards.
She took notes to remind her of the facts.

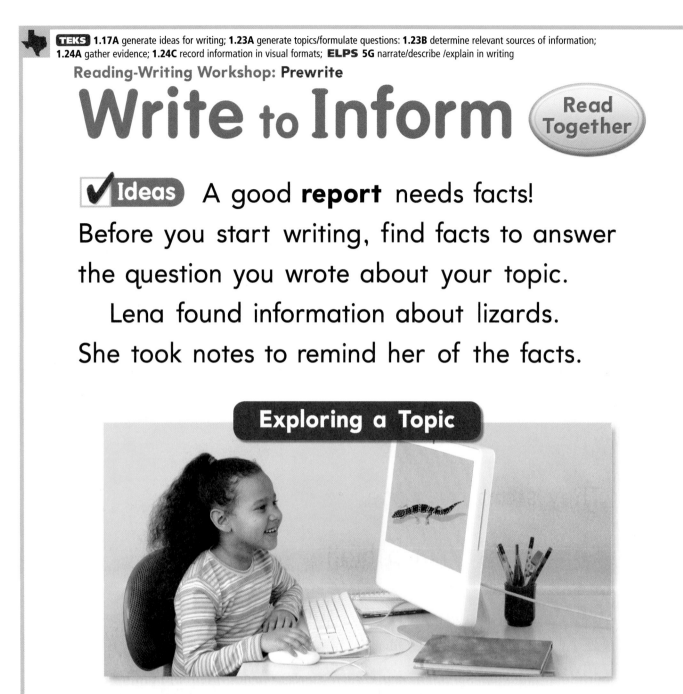

Exploring a Topic

Prewriting Checklist

☑ Did I write a good question about my topic?

☑ Will my notes help me remember the facts?

☑ Did I use good sources for information?

164

Look for facts in Lena's notes. Then record your own notes. Use the Checklist.

Planning Chart

My Question
What do real lizards do?

Fact 1
change color

Fact 2
run fast on back legs

Fact 3
puff up to look big

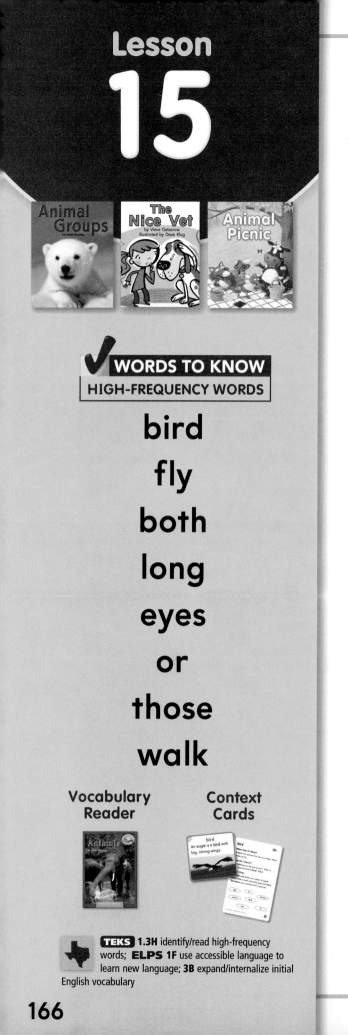

Lesson 15

Animal Groups
by James Bradley

The Nice Vet
by Vince Delacroix
illustrated by Dave Klug

Animal Picnic

✓ WORDS TO KNOW

HIGH-FREQUENCY WORDS

bird

fly

both

long

eyes

or

those

walk

Vocabulary Reader

Context Cards

TEKS 1.3H identify/read high-frequency words; **ELPS** 1F use accessible language to learn new language; **3B** expand/internalize initial English vocabulary

Words to Know

Read Together

● Read each Context Card.

● Ask a question that uses one of the blue words.

1

bird

An eagle is a bird with big, strong wings.

2

fly

Bats are mammals that are able to fly.

3 both
The lizard has both stripes and spots.

4 long
This kangaroo has a long tail.

5 eyes
This dog has blue eyes.

6 or
Ducks can either swim or fly.

7 those
Those fish are not the same colors.

8 walk
The elephants walk together in a group.

TEKS **1.3H** identify/read high-frequency words; **1.6D** categorize words; **RC-1(F)** make connections to experiences/texts/community; **ELPS 4D** use prereading supports to comprehend texts; **4F** use visual/contextual/peer/teacher support to read/comprehend texts

Background

✓ WORDS TO KNOW Animals on the Move

1. A bird will fly, and a fish will swim.

2. Both lions and foxes run.

3. Frogs hop or swim.

4. A giraffe will walk on long legs.

5. A hawk's eyes spot food, and it dives.

6. Those are some ways animals move.

Four Animal Groups

| Reptiles | Fish | Birds | Mammals |

Can you name these animals?

Name more animals in each group

TEKS 1.4C establish purpose/monitor comprehension; **RC-1(A)** establish reading purposes; **ELPS 1E** internalize new basic/academic language; 4F use visual/contextual/peer/teacher support to read/comprehend texts

Comprehension

Read Together

✓ **TARGET SKILL** Compare and Contrast

When you **compare**, tell how things are the same. When you **contrast**, tell how things are different. Good readers think of how things are alike and different to help them understand a story better. How are a dog and a cat alike? How are they different?

As you read **Animal Groups**, think about the ways animals from different groups are the same and different.

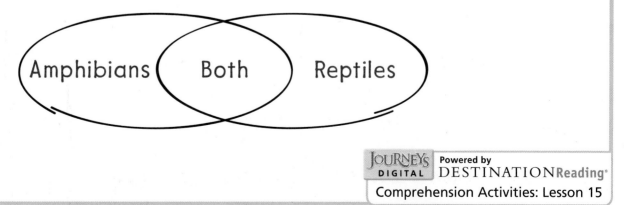

Amphibians   Both   Reptiles

JOURNEYS DIGITAL **Powered by** DESTINATION Reading

Comprehension Activities: Lesson 15

Animal Groups
by James Bruchac

✔ **WORDS TO KNOW**

bird	eyes
fly	or
both	those
long	walk

✔ **TARGET SKILL**

Compare and Contrast
Tell how two things are alike or not.

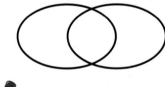

✔ **TARGET STRATEGY**

Monitor/Clarify Find ways to figure out what doesn't make sense.

GENRE
Informational text gives facts on a topic.

TEKS **1.4B** ask questions/seek clarification/ locate details about texts; **1.4C** establish purpose/monitor comprehension; **RC-1(C)** monitor/adjust comprehension **ELPS 4K** employ analytical skills to demonstrate comprehension

Meet the Author

James Bruchac

James Bruchac has many interests. He is a writer, a storyteller, an animal tracker, and a wilderness guide. Together with his father, Joseph Bruchac, he wrote the books **How Chipmunk Got His Stripes** and **Turtle's Race with Beaver**.

Animal Groups

written by James Bruchac

Fish

Amphibian

Reptile

Let's take a look at five animal groups.

Bird

Mammal

How are animals in a group the same?

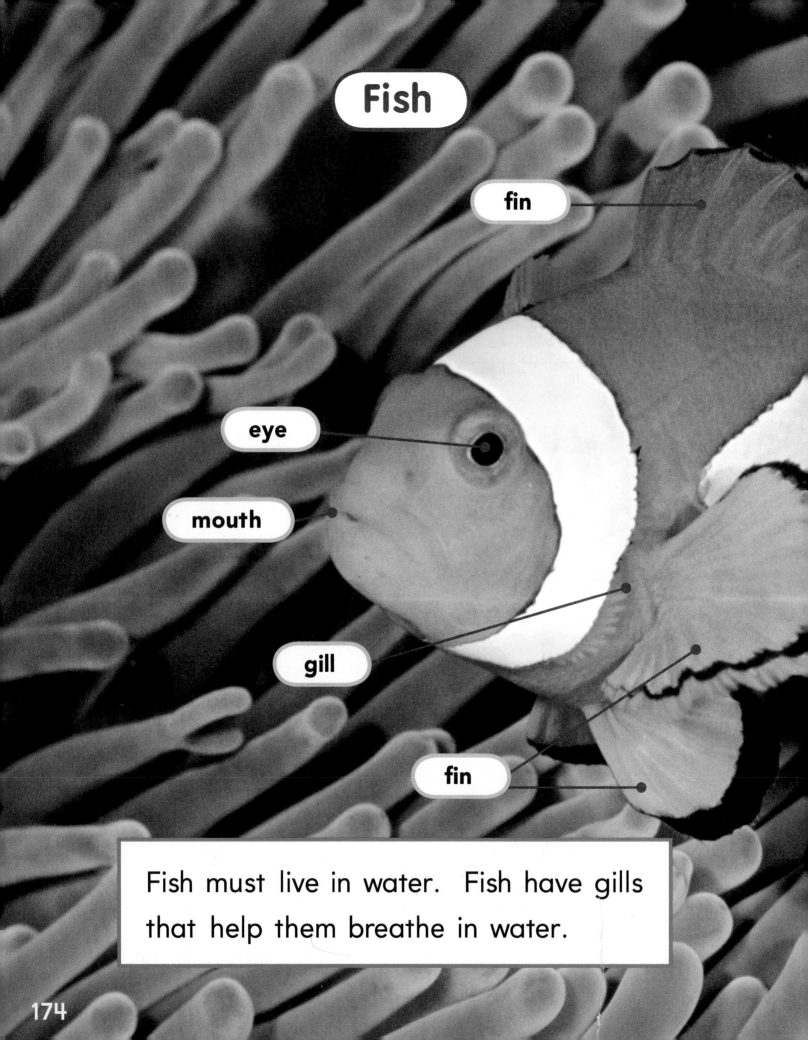

Fish

fin

eye

mouth

gill

fin

Fish must live in water. Fish have gills that help them breathe in water.

174

tail

Fish have fins and tails. Those help them swim.

Fish can be many shapes and sizes.
Can you find a fish in this picture?

Reptiles

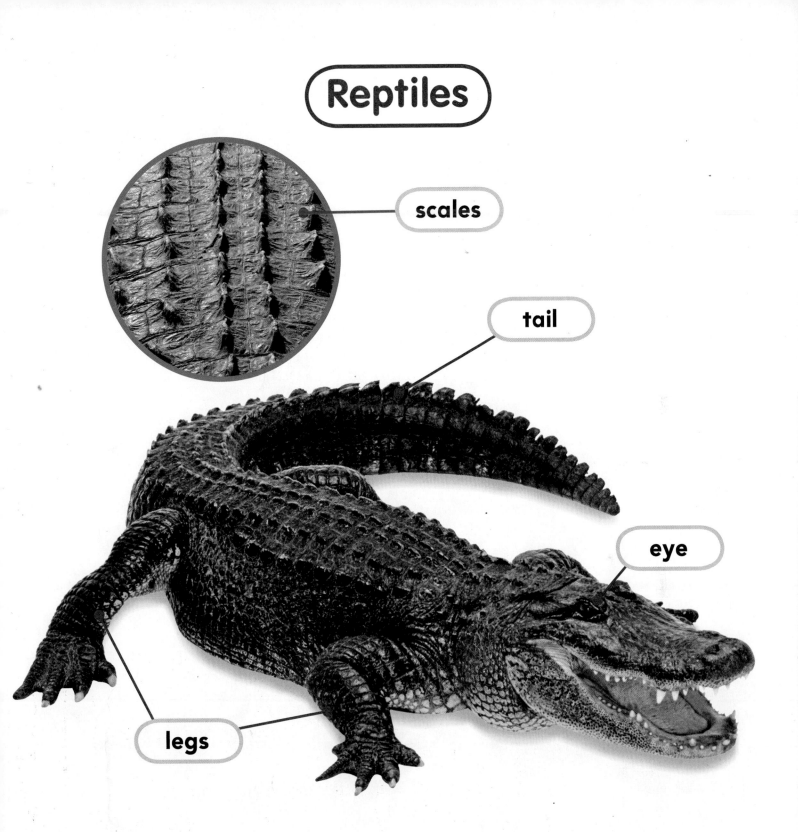

scales

tail

eye

legs

Reptiles can live on land. Some like to be in water. Reptiles have scales on their skin.

Many reptiles hatch from eggs.

Snakes cannot walk. They do not have legs. This snake slides its long body on the grass.

Amphibians

eye

wet skin

legs

Amphibians spend time both on land
and in water. They do not have scales.
Their skin is wet.

tadpoles

Amphibians hatch from eggs.
Tadpoles hatch and grow to be frogs.

Birds

eye

bill

wing

feathers

A bird has feathers and wings. This
bird's eyes are on the sides of its face!

Many birds can fly. Some can run
or swim fast.

Birds hatch from eggs. This hen made a nest for its eggs.

Mammals

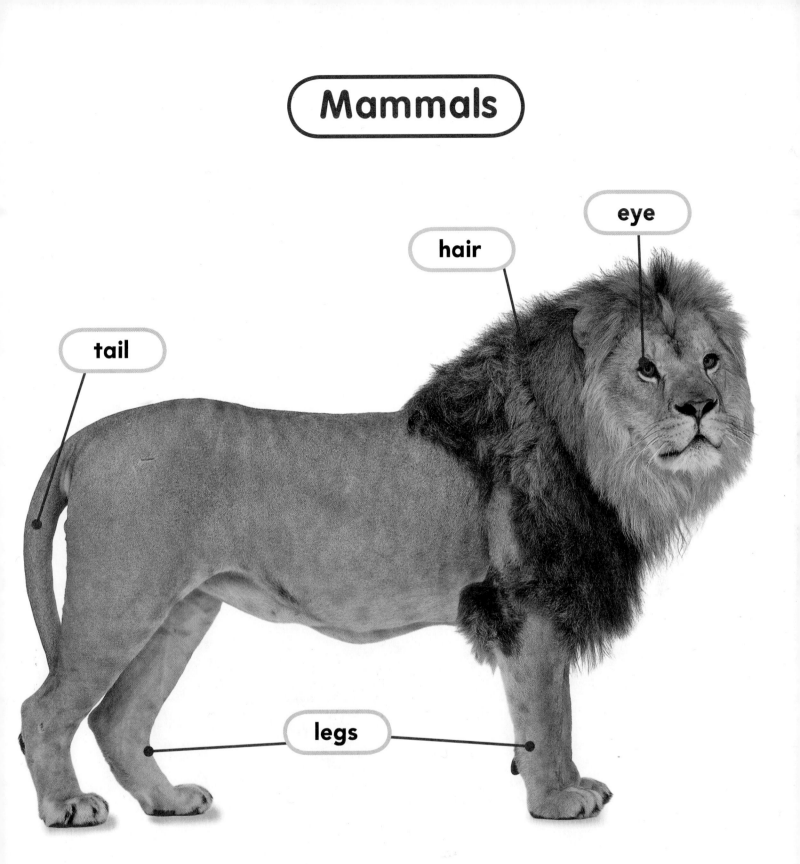

eye

hair

tail

legs

Mammals can be many shapes and sizes.
They have hair on their skin.

A mammal mom can
make milk for its baby.

Lots of mammals live on land,
but some live in water.

Did you know that you are a mammal, too?

Read Together YourTurn

---

1. In the story, the word <u>walk</u> means —

⬭ to move on foot

⬭ to move with wings

⬭ to move with fins and tails

TEKS 1.6C

---

2. ✔ **TARGET SKILL** **Compare and Contrast**

How are amphibians and birds the same?
How are they different? TEKS 1.14B, 1.24C; ELPS 4J

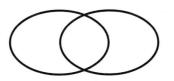

3. Oral Language Work with four
classmates. Each of you choose
an animal group to tell about.
Use the Retelling Cards and
speak clearly. TEKS 1.14B, 1.28

Retelling Cards

TEKS **1.6C** use syntax/context to determine meaning; **1.14B** identify important facts/details; **1.24C** record information in visual formats; **1.28** share information/ideas by speaking clearly; **ELPS 4J** employ inferential skills to demonstrate comprehension

✓ **PHONICS SKILL**

Long **i: i-e**
Digraphs **wr, mb**

✓ **WORDS TO KNOW**

long
eyes
walk

TEKS **1.3A(i)** decode words with consonants; **1.3A(ii)** decode words with vowels; **1.3A(iv)** decode words with consonant digraphs; **1.3C(iv)** decode using VCe pattern; **1.3H** identify/read high-frequency words; **ELPS 4A** learn English sound-letter relationships/decode

The Nice Vet

by Vince Delacroix

illustrated by Dave Klug

Kate's dog Spike has an itch.
Spike rubs and rubs his eyes.
Kate calls Spike's vet.

"Spike has an itch," Kate tells Spike's
vet. "Spike rubs and rubs his eyes."
The vet has time to see Spike.

Spike's vet is nice. Spike likes him.
Spike does not like his itch.

Kate and Spike walk fast.

Kate's mom goes with them.

Spike still has an itch.

Spike whines and whines.

At last, they get to the vet's place.
It's not a long walk.
"I can fix Spike's itch," the vet tells
Kate. "I will make his eyes numb."

Spike's vet puts five drops in Spike's
eyes. Spike's eyes stop itching!
The vet writes in Spike's file.

Kate hands Spike's vet a dime.
Nice price, isn't it? Who is
Spike's nice vet? It's Kate's dad!

Connect to Plays

✔ WORDS TO KNOW

bird	eyes
fly	or
both	those
long	walk

GENRE

A **play** is a story that people act out.

TEXT FOCUS

Stage directions in plays tell about the characters and setting.

TEKS 1.3H identify/read high-frequency words; **ELPS** 4F use visual/contextual/peer/ teacher support to read/comprehend texts

Animal Picnic

by Debbie O'Brien

Cast of Characters

Fox

Cow

Bird

 Hi, Cow and Bird. How was your trip?

 I had to walk to get here.

 I had to fly.

(pointing to Cow's basket)
What food did you bring for
our picnic?

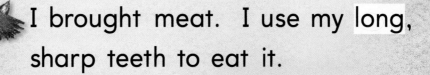 I brought grass. I use my flat
teeth to grind it.

I brought meat. I use my long,
sharp teeth to eat it.

We both have teeth, but we
eat different things!

(pointing to Bird's basket)
What did you bring, Bird?

199

I did not bring grass or meat.
I brought seeds. Birds don't
have any teeth!

 How will you eat those seeds
without teeth?

Keep your eyes on me!
(Bird eats some seeds.)
Yum, yum, yum!

Making Connections

Read Together

Animal Groups
by James Bruchac

Animal Picnic

Text to Self

TEKS 1.27A, 1.29, RC-1(F)

Talk About Animals Which animal group is your favorite? Which animal group did you learn the most about? Discuss with a partner.

Text to Text

TEKS 1.19A, RC-1(F)

Connect to Language Arts Choose an animal from **Animal Groups**. Then think about **Animal Picnic**. Write what that animal might say and do at the picnic.

Text to World

TEKS 1.23A, 1.23B, RC-1(F)

List Questions Think of an animal you would like to know more about. List questions you have about the animal. Where could you find the answers?

TEKS 1.19A write brief compositions; **1.23A** generate topics/formulate questions; **1.23B** determine relevant sources of information; **1.27A** listen attentively/ask relevant questions; **1.29** follow discussion rules; **RC-1(F)** make connections to experiences/texts/community; **ELPS 1E** internalize new basic/academic language; **2G** understand meaning/main points/details of spoken language; **3G** express opinions/ideas/feelings

Grammar

The Verb **be** The verbs **is** and **are** tell what is happening now. Use **is** with a noun that names one.

One	More Than One

This **chick** is small.	Two **chicks** are small.

The verbs **was** and **were** tell what happened in the past. Use **was** with a noun that names one.

One	More Than One
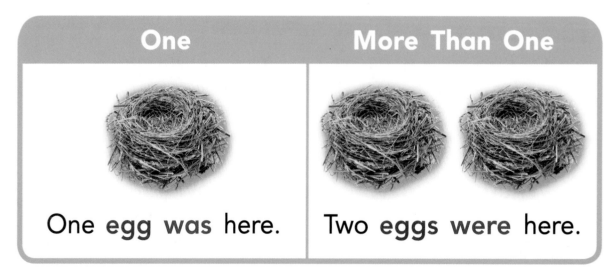	
One **egg** was here.	Two **eggs** were here.

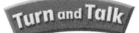

Read each sentence aloud two times, saying a different verb each time. Ask your partner to repeat the sentence with the correct verb. Then switch roles.

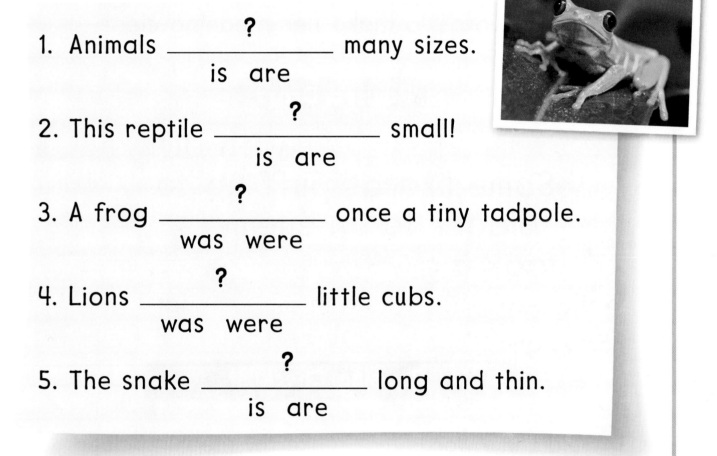

1. Animals _____ many sizes.
   ?
   is   are

2. This reptile _____ small!
   ?
   is   are

3. A frog _____ once a tiny tadpole.
   ?
   was   were

4. Lions _____ little cubs.
   ?
   was   were

5. The snake _____ long and thin.
   ?
   is   are

Grammar in Writing

When you proofread your writing, be sure you have used the verbs **is**, **are**, **was**, and **were** correctly.

TEKS 1.17C revise drafts; 1.17D edit drafts; 1.19A write brief compositions; **ELPS 5C** spell English words with increasing accuracy; **5D** edit writing for standard grammar/usage; **5G** narrate/describe/explain in writing

Reading-Writing Workshop: Revise

Write to Inform

Read Together

✔ **Word Choice**   In a good **report**, the right words make the facts easy to understand.

Lena drafted her report. Later, she wrote different words to make her meaning clear.

Revised Draft

with air

Some lizards puff up ^ to

bigger to an enemy

look ~~big~~.

^

 Revising Checklist

✔ Did I use words that make my meaning clear?

✔ Did I use correct punctuation?

✔ Did I spell words correctly?

TEKS 1.17C revise drafts; 1.17D edit drafts; 1.19A write brief compositions; **ELPS 5C** spell English words with increasing accuracy; **5D** edit writing for standard grammar/usage; **5G** narrate/describe/explain in writing

Look for exact words in Lena's final copy.
Then revise your writing. Use the Checklist.

Final Copy

An Interesting Reptile

Lizards do some funny things.

Some can change color quickly.

Others run fast using only their

back legs. Some lizards

puff up with air to look

bigger to an enemy.

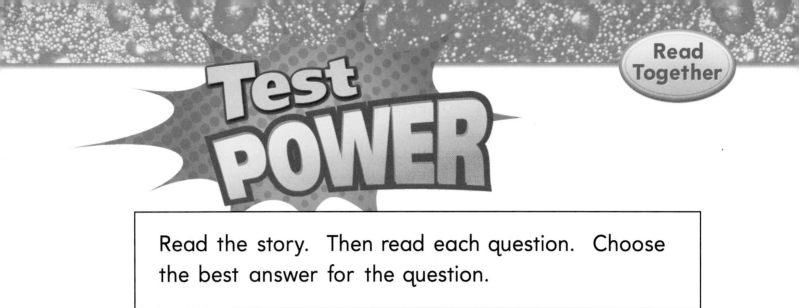

Test POWER

Read the story. Then read each question. Choose the best answer for the question.

Frogs and Toads

Frogs and toads are alike in some ways. They both lay eggs in water. They both live in water when they are small. They both eat lots of bugs.

Frogs and toads are different in some ways, too. Frogs have smooth, wet skin. Frogs live in or near water. They have long back legs, too. This helps them hop and swim.

Toads have <u>dry</u>, bumpy skin. Toads spend much of their time on land. They have small back legs. This helps them walk.

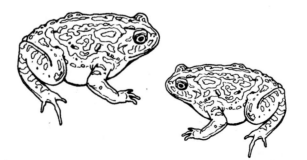

1 Why did the author write this?

- ⬭ To tell a funny story
- ⬭ To give facts
- ⬭ To tell you what to do

2 How are frogs different from toads?

- ⬭ Frogs lay eggs in water.
- ⬭ Frogs eat bugs.
- ⬭ Frogs have smooth, wet skin.

3 Which word from the story means the opposite of <u>dry</u>?

- ⬭ Bumpy
- ⬭ Wet
- ⬭ Long

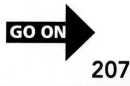
GO ON

Roly-Poly Bugs

A pill bug is also called a roly-poly. It is a very small animal. It can roll into a little ball that looks like a pill. This helps to keep it safe from <u>danger</u>. Pill bugs live where it is damp.

Many people think pill bugs are insects. They are not. A pill bug has fourteen legs, not six. It is in the same family as a crab!

1   Pill bugs get their name because they —
   ⬭ have many legs
   ⬭ are made of pills
   ⬭ can roll into little balls

2   How are pill bugs different from insects?
   ⬭ They have six legs.
   ⬭ They have fourteen legs.
   ⬭ They are small.

3   The word <u>danger</u> means —
   ⬭ safety
   ⬭ help
   ⬭ harm

STOP

POWER Practice

Sorting Words

Read Together

You can group words that are alike.

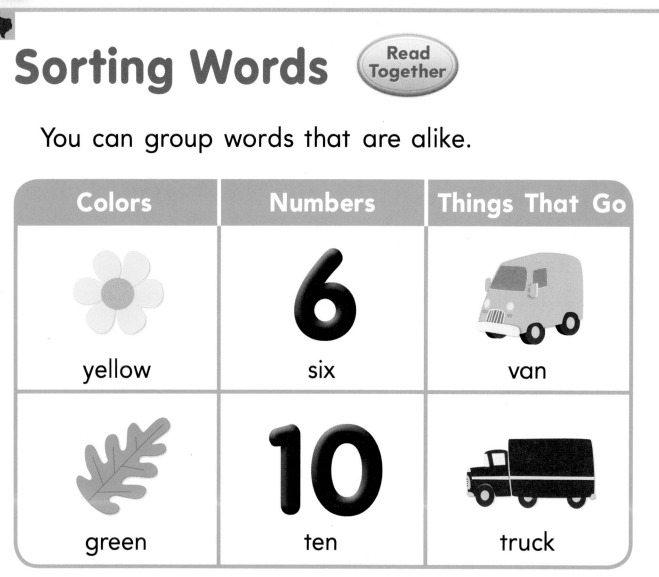

Colors	Numbers	Things That Go
yellow	six	van
green	ten	truck

1. Make a chart like this one. Use another sheet of paper.

Colors	Numbers	Things That Go

TEKS 1.6D categorize words

2. Think about the words in this box. Some words belong on the chart you made and some do not.

red	car	bus	one
circle	pink	two	triangle

3. Sort each of the words and write them in the correct group on your chart.

4. Which words are left over? What group do they belong to?

Add more words to your chart.

Spelling

Read Together

You can add the letter **s** to a root word to make a new word.

Add **s** to **cat**.

I have one **cat**.

Kim has two **cats**.

Add **s** to **help**.

I **help** Dad.

Dad **helps** me.

TEKS **1.21A** form letters legibly; **1.22D** spell words with inflectional endings

Write each word below on a sheet of paper. Use your best handwriting. Check that the letters are formed correctly.

pin	nap	sing	cup
trick	mop	want	tap
pet	flip	like	hand

Write each word again. Add **s** to the end.

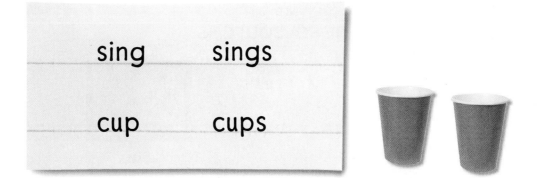

sing	sings
cup	cups

Read all the words you have written.

Write a sentence using a word with **s** at the end.

TEKS 1.24A gather evidence

Research Read Together

When you **gather information** for a research report, you collect facts about your topic from different sources.

You can get information by reading these sources.

encyclopedias   magazines
nonfiction books   Internet sites

You can learn about your topic by watching and visiting these sources.

movies
TV shows
museums

You can get information directly from people, too.

listen to a speaker
interview a person

Do your own research. Think of a pet you would like to have. Pick a good source to learn about that pet. You might read a book, a magazine story, or an encyclopedia article. Take notes about what you learn.

Do more research about that pet. Interview a family member, a friend, or a neighbor who owns that kind of pet. Ask questions. Take notes about the answers to your questions.

Interviews

Read
Together

A research report answers questions about a topic. Sometimes there are experts who know a lot about the topic. You can **gather information** for your research report by talking to experts about a subject.

Think of something you want to know more about. Make a chart like this to help organize your thoughts about your topic:

What I Know	Questions I Have

TEKS 1.24A gather evidence

Now think of someone at home or at school you could interview about your topic to get more information. Use this information to help you talk to your expert.

Before the interview:

- Make a list of questions you want to ask.

- Write them down neatly.

During the interview:

- Ask the expert your questions.

- Speak clearly and use complete sentences.

- Write down your expert's answers.

After the interview:

- Thank your expert for helping you.

When does the robin build its nest? How long does it take for the eggs to hatch?

Writing a Letter

You can write a letter to tell someone how to do something. When you write a letter, be sure you have all the parts.

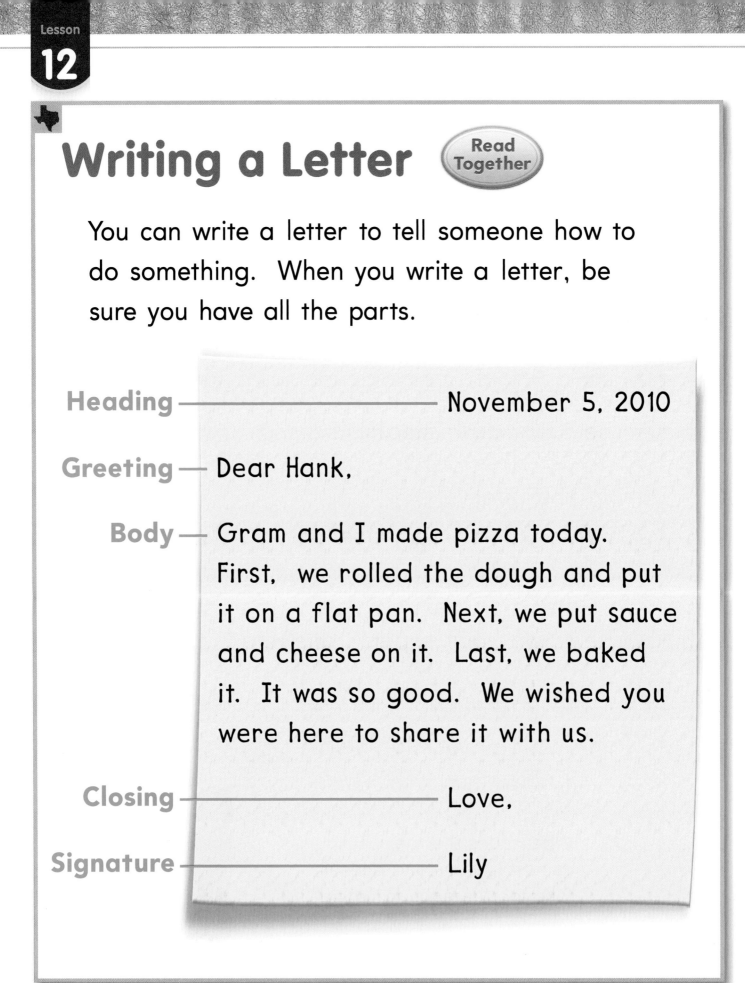

Heading ———————— November 5, 2010

Greeting — Dear Hank,

Body — Gram and I made pizza today. First, we rolled the dough and put it on a flat pan. Next, we put sauce and cheese on it. Last, we baked it. It was so good. We wished you were here to share it with us.

Closing ———————— Love,

Signature ———————— Lily

TEKS 1.19B write short letters; 1.20A(vii) understand/use time-order transition words

Write a letter to a friend. Tell how to do or make something. Be sure to give the instructions in order. Use words like **first**, **next**, and **last** to make your writing clear. Remember to use the five parts of a letter. When you are finished, read your letter to a partner.

Ask Questions

You ask questions to get information or to find out more about something. You can also ask a question to make sure you understood something. When you ask a question, a question word or a verb often comes first. The words in the answer often change order.

Question	Answer
What **is** his favorite **animal**?	His favorite **animal is** a snake.
Where **is** the **book**?	The **book is** in the library.
Does she have a dog?	**She does** have a dog.
Can I jump far?	**I can** jump far.

TEKS **1.4B** ask questions/seek clarification/locate details about texts; **1.20C** ask questions with subject-verb inversion

Think about the story events in **How Leopard Got His Spots**. Write two questions about things you did not understand in the story. Trade papers with a partner. Write answers to your partner's questions.

Spelling

Remember that you can add the letter **s** to a root word to make a new word.

Add **s** to **spot.**

This dog has one **spot**.

This dog has many **spots**.

Add **s** to **follow.**

I **follow** Sam.

Meg **follows** me.

TEKS **1.21A** form letters legibly; **1.22D** spell words with inflectional endings

Write each word below on a sheet of paper. Use your best handwriting. Check that the letters are formed correctly.

swing	plant	track	hat
rock	run	spoon	forest
pat	goat	make	stand

Write each word again. Add **s** to the end.

run	runs
spoon	spoons

Read all the words you have written.

Write a sentence using a word with **s** at the end.

Gathering Information

Read Together

When you **gather information** for a research report, you collect facts about your topic. You can gather information from different sources.

- books and magazines
- movies and the Internet
- people who know a lot about the topic

TEKS 1.24A gather evidence

How could you find out about all the animals in your neighborhood? Work with a partner.

1. Make a list of all the animals you have seen in your neighborhood. Write what you know about them.

2. Think of people who might know about animals in your neighborhood. Ask them for more information. Write it down.

3. Think about books or magazines that could give you more information. Take notes on what you read.

4. Are there any other sources of information? Use them to find out as much as you can about animals in your neighborhood.

Handwriting

Read Together

Trace each letter with your finger. Then write each letter on a sheet of writing paper.

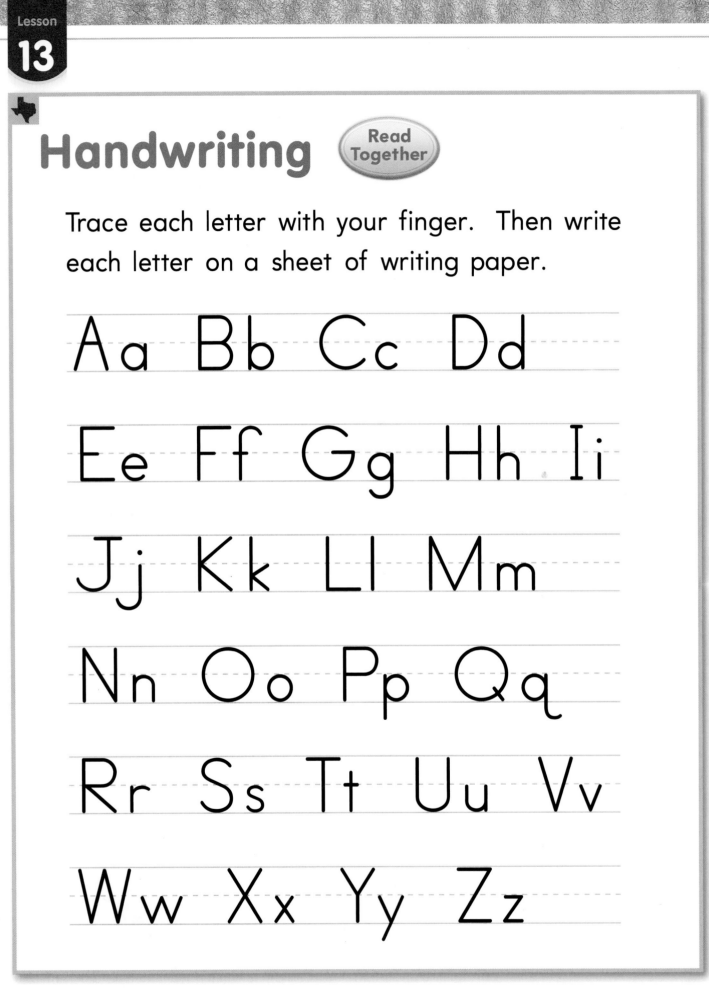

Aa Bb Cc Dd

Ee Ff Gg Hh Ii

Jj Kk Ll Mm

Nn Oo Pp Qq

Rr Ss Tt Uu Vv

Ww Xx Yy Zz

TEKS 1.21A form letters legibly

Now practice writing the words below. Make sure your letters are not too close together or too far apart.

bug

play

spot

forest

sing

Write this sentence on your paper.
Leave enough space between each word
so that your sentence is easy to read.

I want to climb the tallest

tree in the forest.

Gathering Information

Read Together

When you **gather information** for a research report, you collect facts about a topic from different sources.

Think about different things you would like to learn about seasons. Then choose one topic. You can use resources to find information about your topic.

snowflake

winter in my town

raindrop

when it rains

thermometer

when it's hot

Think of questions you have about your topic. Then decide where you can find answers to your questions. A chart can help.

TEKS 1.24A gather evidence

Questions	Sources for Information	Answers
What is the hottest season?	Ask Gram. Look in an almanac. Call a weather station.	
How hot can it get in my town?	Look in the newspaper. Ask a local weather forecaster.	

Make a chart.

1. In the first column, write questions you have about your topic.

2. In the second column, make a list of sources that will help you find answers.

3. Use your sources to get information.

4. In the third column, write what you have learned about your topic.

Spelling *Read Together*

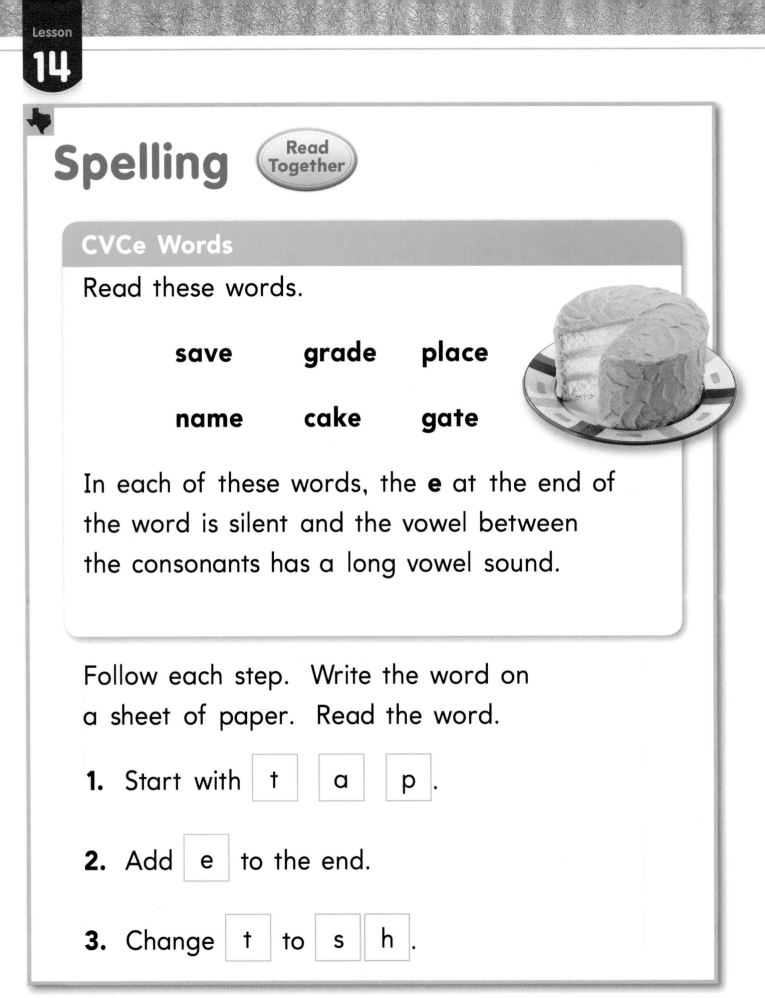

CVCe Words

Read these words.

save	**grade**	**place**
name	**cake**	**gate**

In each of these words, the **e** at the end of the word is silent and the vowel between the consonants has a long vowel sound.

Follow each step. Write the word on a sheet of paper. Read the word.

1. Start with t a p .

2. Add e to the end.

3. Change t to s h .

TEKS 1.3B apply letter-sound knowledge to create words; 1.21A form letters legibly; 1.22B(ii) spell CVCe words

4. Change | s | h | to | c | .

5. Change | p | to | k | .

6. Change | c | to | r | .

7. Change | k | to | c | .

Handwriting

Read Together

Write the sentences neatly on a sheet of paper.
Form the letters carefully.
Put a pencil space between
each word. Put two pencil
spaces between the sentences.

The animals had a big race.
Can you name who won?

Using Resources

Dictionaries

A **dictionary** helps you find the meaning of a word. It also helps you check the spelling.

Words in a dictionary are in ABC order.

R

rabbit an animal with long ears

race a contest to see who is fastest

radish a vegetable

Work with a partner. You can use a dictionary to help you find these words. You can use the dictionary to help you spell the words correctly.

TEKS **1.1F** identify information provided by book parts; **1.6E** alphabetize/use dictionary; **1.22E** use resources to find correct spellings

1. Write a word you would find in the dictionary before the word **banana**.

2. Write a word you would find in the dictionary after the word **rain**.

Glossaries

Some books have a glossary at the end. Glossaries are like dictionaries. A glossary tells the meanings of words that you find in the book. A glossary also shows the correct spelling of a word.

race a contest to see who is fastest

run to move quickly by foot

Use the glossary in this book to find three words you want to use in your writing. Write them carefully. Then write sentences using the words.

Research

Read Together

Using a Table of Contents

A **table of contents** tells the page number on which each part of a book begins. You can use a table of contents to help you find information in a book quickly.

Table of Contents

TEKS **1.1F** identify information provided by book parts; **1.24B** use text features to locate information

Answer these questions on a sheet of paper.

1. On which page does Chapter 1 begin?

2. Which chapter begins on page 23?

3. What is the title of Chapter 2?

4. If you want to learn about animals of the Arctic, which page would you turn to?

 Try This!

Find the Table of Contents in this book.
Point to the title of the story you just read.
Read the title. To read the story again, what page would you turn to?

Publishing

You can publish your report in a class book.

Copy your report neatly. Draw pictures to go with it.

You can make a class book out of all the reports.

Sharks

Sharks live in the sea. They have lots of teeth.

Make a Book

- Punch holes in the sides of the reports.

- Tie the reports together with yarn.

- Decide on a title, and make a book cover.

- Write the title on the cover.

TEKS **1.17E** publish/share writing; **1.29** follow discussion rules

Sharing

After you and your classmates have finished the class book, take turns sharing it with each other. Follow these rules for discussion.

- Look at the person who is talking.

- Listen carefully.

- Raise your hand. Wait to be called on to talk.

- Stay on topic when you speak.

- Speak clearly.

- Do not speak too quickly or too slowly.

- Speak in complete sentences.

Sea Animals

Spelling

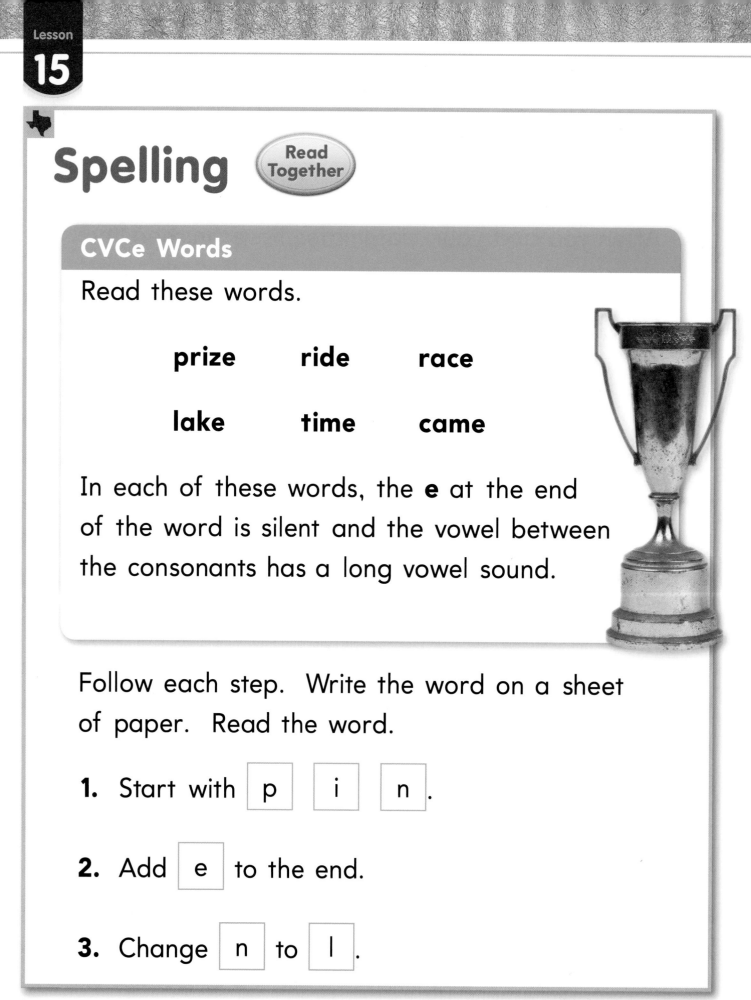

Read Together

CVCe Words

Read these words.

prize   **ride**   **race**

lake   **time**   **came**

In each of these words, the **e** at the end of the word is silent and the vowel between the consonants has a long vowel sound.

Follow each step. Write the word on a sheet of paper. Read the word.

1. Start with ⬚p⬚ ⬚i⬚ ⬚n⬚.

2. Add ⬚e⬚ to the end.

3. Change ⬚n⬚ to ⬚l⬚.

TEKS **1.3B** apply letter-sound knowledge to create words; **1.21A** form letters legibly; **1.22B(ii)** spell CVCe words

4. Change p to m .

5. Change l to n .

6. Change m to v .

Handwriting

Write the sentences below neatly on a sheet of paper. Form the letters carefully. Put a pencil space between each word. Put two pencil spaces between the sentences.

I have to take my puppy to the vet. I hope she is fine.

Using an Index

Read Together

An **index** helps you find information in a book. You can find an index in the back of a book.

- The subjects are listed in ABC order.

- The page numbers are listed next to each subject.

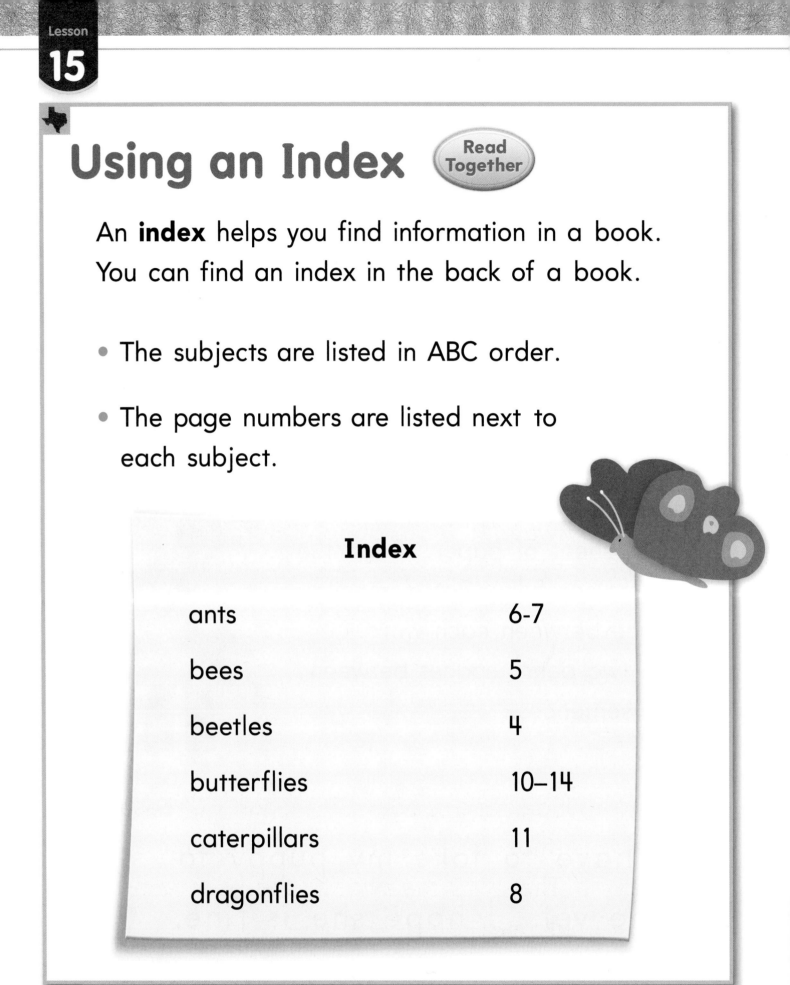

Index

ants	6-7
bees	5
beetles	4
butterflies	10–14
caterpillars	11
dragonflies	8

TEKS 1.1F identify information provided by book parts; 1.24B use text features to locate information

Use the Index on page 240 to answer these questions on a sheet of paper.

1. On which page could you read about dragonflies?

2. What will you learn about if you turn to pages 6 and 7?

3. Where could you find out about bees?

4. If you want to learn about caterpillars, which page would you turn to?

Find the index in the back of a book. Choose a subject that interests you. Find the page number. Then find the page in the book and read about the subject.

Using a Dictionary

Read Together

A **dictionary** helps you find information. It tells you the meaning of words.

Words in the dictionary are in ABC order.

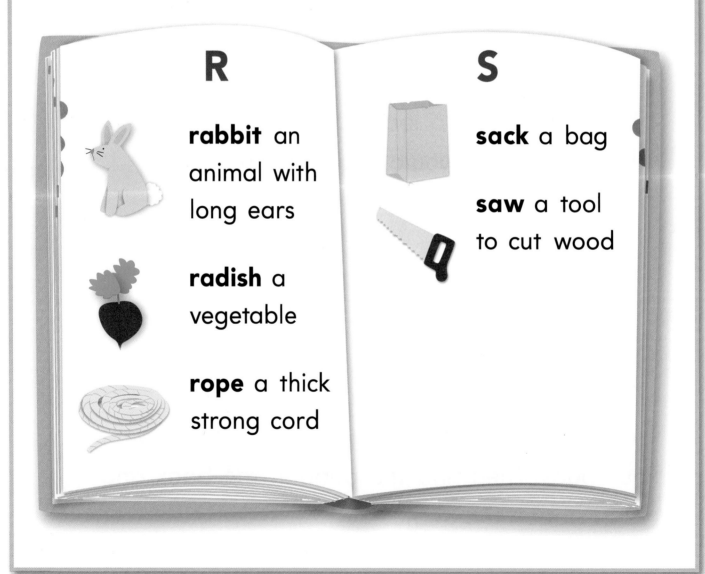

R

rabbit an animal with long ears

radish a vegetable

rope a thick strong cord

S

sack a bag

saw a tool to cut wood

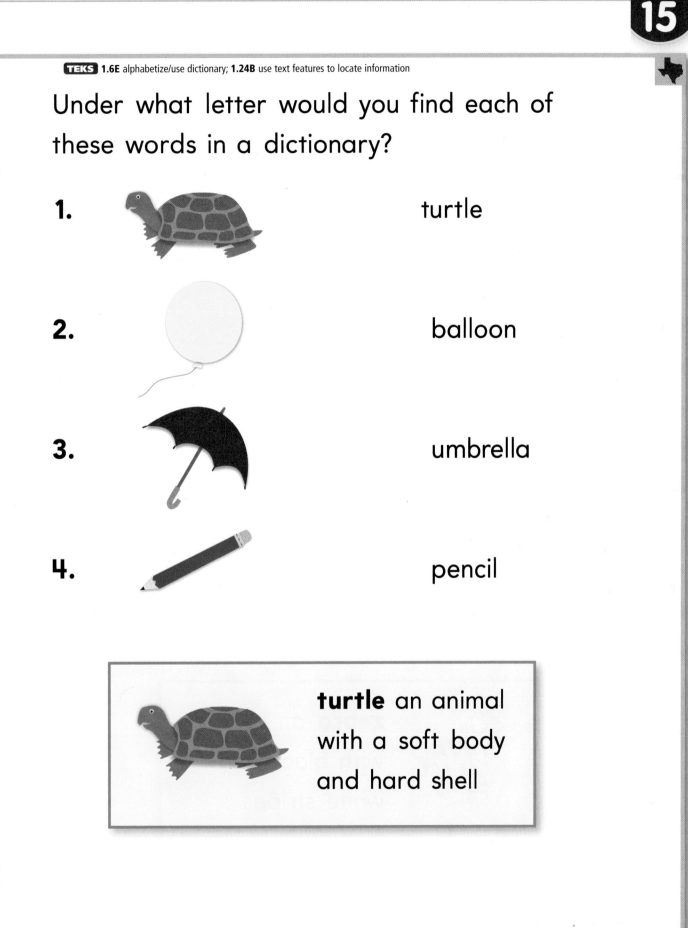

TEKS 1.6E alphabetize/use dictionary; 1.24B use text features to locate information

Under what letter would you find each of these words in a dictionary?

1. turtle

2. balloon

3. umbrella

4. pencil

turtle an animal with a soft body and hard shell

Under what letter would you find each of these words in a dictionary?

5.  king

6. drum

Work with a partner. Choose a word and look it up in a dictionary. Read the meaning together.

 **zebra** an animal with black and white stripes

Words to Know

Unit 3 High-Frequency Words

⑪ Sea Animals

cold	far
where	their
blue	little
live	water

⑭ The Big Race

two	over
into	four
three	five
starts	watch

⑫ How Leopard Got His Spots

brown	never
own	know
very	out
off	been

⑮ Animal Groups

bird	eyes
fly	or
both	those
long	walk

⑬ Seasons

green	fall
yellow	new
grow	down
open	goes

Glossary

A

amphibians

An **amphibian** is an animal that lives in water and on land. Frogs are **amphibians**.

B

blow

To **blow** means to push air. The winds **blow** the cold air across the land.

body

The **body** of a person or animal is made up of the parts you can see and touch. We are learning about the parts of the **body**.

breathe

To **breathe** is to take in breaths of air. I **breathe** in the fresh air when I am outside.

C

cottontail

A **cottontail** is a kind of rabbit. That **cottontail** has a white fluffy tail.

D

danced

To **dance** means to move to music. We played music and **danced** for hours.

day

A **day** is the time from one morning to the next morning. Tuesday was a sunny **day**.

F

feathers

A **feather** is a part of a bird. The bird had soft feathers.

fish

A **fish** is an animal that lives in water. My uncle has a yellow **fish** with black stripes.

flippers

A **flipper** is a kind of arm that helps an animal swim. The seal used its **flippers** to move in the water.

flowers

A **flower** is a part of a plant. We planted pretty **flowers** in the garden.

G

giraffe

A **giraffe** is a tall spotted animal with a long neck. The **giraffe** ate leaves from the top of the tree.

group

A **group** is a number of people or things together. A **group** of us went swimming last Saturday.

H

hair

Hair is what grows on your head. My dad cuts my **hair** when it gets too long.

hay

Hay is a kind of grass that has been cut and dried. My horse likes to eat **hay**.

home

A **home** is a place where people or animals live. Jellyfish make their **home** underwater.

hooray

Hooray is something people shout when they are happy. When I hit a home run, my parents yelled **hooray!**

hyena

A **hyena** is a wild animal that looks like a dog. The **hyena** is found in Africa and Asia.

L

leaves

A **leaf** is a part of a plant. In the fall, the **leaves** turn pretty colors.

leopard

A **leopard** is a wild animal that looks like a cat with spots. The **leopard** paced in its cage.

lions

A **lion** is a large wild animal that looks like a big cat. We saw a movie about **lions** in Africa.

lizard

A **lizard** is a small reptile. The **lizard** lay on the rock in the hot sun.

M

mammals

A **mammal** is a warm-blooded animal. Cats are **mammals**.

P

paints

To **paint** means to cover something with color. My Aunt Carly **paints** houses.

penguins

A **penguin** is a kind of bird that lives in cold places. **Penguins** keep their chicks warm.

pink

Pink is a very light shade of red. My sister painted her nails **pink**.

R

race

A **race** is a contest to find out who is the fastest. Selena got to the finish line first and won the **race**.

reptiles

A **reptile** is a cold-blooded animal. Snakes are **reptiles**.

roadrunner

A **roadrunner** is a very fast bird. We saw a **roadrunner** in the Arizona desert.

S

school

A **school** is a place where students learn from teachers. My best friend and I go to the same **school**.

sea

A **sea** is a big body of water. The **sea** is filled with all kinds of fish.

sea lions

A **sea lion** is a large seal that lives by the ocean. **Sea lions** swim and then rest up on the rocks.

sea stars

A **sea star** is an ocean animal with long arms and hard skin. **Sea stars** are also called <u>starfish</u>.

seeds

A **seed** is a part of a plant. Most plants grow from tiny little **seeds**.

snow
Snow is tiny pieces of frozen water that fall from the clouds. When we woke up, the ground was covered with **snow**.

snowman
A **snowman** looks like a person made of snow. We piled three balls of snow on top of each other and made a **snowman**.

spring
Spring is the season that comes after winter. In the **spring**, the flowers begin to bloom.

summer
Summer is the season that comes after spring. This **summer** my family will go to the beach.

T

tadpoles
A **tadpole** is a baby frog. I found **tadpoles** swimming in our pond.

tails
A **tail** is a part of some animals' bodies. Rats have long **tails**.

tall

To be **tall** is to stand high above the ground. The giraffe is very **tall**.

turtle

A **turtle** is a reptile with a shell. The **turtle** went inside its shell as soon as I touched it.

W

warm

Warm means not very hot. The tea was still **warm** after it sat for a while.

wings

A **wing** is a part that helps something to fly. The bird flapped its **wings** and flew away.

winter

Winter is a season that comes after fall. Last **winter** was very cold!

Z

zebra

A **zebra** is a striped animal that looks like a horse. My favorite animal is the **zebra**.

Acknowledgments

"Listen" by Margaret Hillert. Reprinted by
permission of the author who controls all rights.
"Spring Song" from *Seasons: A Book of Poems*
by Charlotte Zolotow. Copyright © 2002 by
Charlotte Zolotow. Reprinted by permission of
HarperCollins Publishers.

Credits

Photo Credits
Placement Key: (t) top, (b) bottom, (r) right, (l)
left, (bg) background, (fg) foreground, (i) inset

TOC 4 ©Stephen Frink/Getty Images; (br) ©2007
PunchStock; **TOC 8** ©blickwinkell/Alamy; **TOC 8a**
(c) ©Alaska Stock LLC/Alamy; **TOC 8b** Spread
©age fotostock/SuperStock; **9** (tc) ©Alaska
Stock LLC/Alamy; **10** (t) ©Konrad Wothe/
Minden Pictures; (b) ©Reinhard Dirscherl/
AGE FotoStock; **11** (tl) ©Amanda Friedman/
Stone/Getty Images; (tr) ©Ron Sanford/Corbis;
(cl) ©George Grall/National Geographic/
Getty Images; (cr) ©Stockbyte; (bl) ©Getty;
(br) ©Purestock/Getty Images; **12-13** ©Fred
Bavendam/Getty Images; **14** (inset) ©Norbert Wu
Productions; **14-15** ©Norbert Wu Productions;
16 ©Norbert Wu Productions; **17** ©Norbert Wu
Productions; **18** ©Norbert Wu Productions; **19**
©Norbert Wu Productions; **20** ©Norbert Wu
Productions; **21** ©Norbert Wu Productions; **22**
©Norbert Wu Productions; **23** ©Norbert Wu
Productions; **24** ©Norbert Wu Productions; **25**
©Norbert Wu Productions; **26** ©Norbert Wu
Productions; **27** ©Norbert Wu Productions; **28**
©Norbert Wu Productions; **29** ©Norbert Wu
Productions; **30** ©Norbert Wu Productions; **40** (c)
©Lew Robertson/Getty Images; **41** (bg) ©Siede
Preis; **42** (bg) ©Photodisc/Cybermedia; **43** inset
©Andres Stapff/Reuters/Corbis; **44** (c) ©George
Grail/Getty Images; **45** (tl) ©Johnny Johnson/
Getty Images; (cl) ©Vittorio Sciosia/Alamy; (bl)

©Roger Tidman/Corbis; (tr) ©Jose B. Ruiz/
naturepl.com; (cr) ©Robert Brenner/PhotoEdit;
48 (t) ©Photodisc; (b) © 1997 PhotoDisc, Inc.
All rights reserved. Images provided by © 1997
Alan D. Carey; **49** (tl) ©Design Pics Inc./Alamy;
(tr) ©Roger Tidman/Corbis; (cl) ©Ann & Steve
Toon/Robert Harding World Imagery/Getty
Images ; (cr) ©Gallo Images/Alamy; (bl) ©Rainer
Jahns/Alamy; (br) ©Tom Nebbia/Corbis; **50**
(tl) ©pbnj productions/Brand X/Corbis; **80-81**
©Tony Craddock/Photo Researchers, Inc.; **83**
©Wayne Barret/Corbis; **86** (t) ©Andrew Duke/
Alamy; (b) ©Stock Connection Distribution/
Alamy; **87** (tl) ©Darrell Gulin/Corbis; (tr) ©Jean
Louis Bellurget/Stock Image/Jupiterimages;
(cl) ©Pete Turner/The Image Bank/Getty
Images; (cr) ©Ryan McVay/Taxi/Getty Images;
(bl) ©VEER Gildo Spadoni/Photonica/Getty
Images; (br) ©Steve Mason/PhotoDisc/Getty
Images; **88** ©Willy Matheisl/Alamy; **89** ©Richard
Hutchings/Photo Edit; **90** (inset) ©Courtesy
of Pat Cummings; **91** Spread ©J.A. Kraulis/
Masterfile; **92-93** Spread ©2007 Masterfile
Corporation; **94** (c) ©Bill Leaman/Dembinsky
Photo; **95** ©Richard Hutchings/Photo Edit;
96-97 ©2007 Jupiterimages; **98** ©Masterfile;
99 (t) ©2007 Masterfile Corporation; **100-101**
©2007 Masterfile Corporation; **102** ©Garry
Black/Masterile; **103** (t) ©2007 PunchStock;
104-105 ©Tim Pannell/Corbis; **106** (c)
©George McCarthy/naturepl.com; **107** ©2007
PunchStock; **108** (t) ©2007 PunchStock; (ct)
©Richard Hutchings/Photo Edit; (cb) ©BrandX;
(b) ©2007 PunchStock; **118** ©Darrell Gulin/
Corbis; **118-119** ©Ariel Skelley/Corbis; **120**
©Willy Matheisl/Alamy; **123** ©Darrell Gulin/
Corbis; **126** (t) ©ARCO/H Reinhard; (b) © John
Foxx/Stockbyte/Getty Images; **127** (tl) ©Danita
Delimont/Alamy; (tr) ©Larry Brownstein/
Photodisc; (cl) ©Photos.com; (cr) ©Jonathan
Blair/Corbis; (bl) ©QT Luong/Terragalleria;
(br) ©franzfoto.com/Alamy; **128** ©Don Mason/
Corbis; **130** ©Courtesy of Viviana Garafoli; **131**
©Courtesy of Pam Munoz; **150-151** © Juniors
Bildarchiv/Alamy; **152** © Eastcott Momatiuk/